The Girls of Huntington House

THE

GIRLS

OF

HUNTINGTON

HOUSE

Blossom Elfman

85-528

Houghton Mifflin Company Boston

TO THE MEMORY OF
GUY ENDORE

·

*"And gladly would he learn,
and gladly teach."*

Author's Note

This book was written from the memory of an unusual teaching year. But since the essence of a maternity home is privacy, no privacy shall be violated. All of the characters are composites. What remains unalterable, and unaltered, are the verities of the human heart.

Contents

The Girls of Huntington House

Bid the Boys Goodbye

If it weren't for Mr. Vanderveld's asthma I might never have come to Huntington House. I certainly never applied to teach there. I was solicited. And I accepted the assignment not so much with enthusiasm as out of desperation. Yet, when the semester ended and Doris asked me in that voice of hers, "I don't suppose you expect to return in the fall?" my intention was as clear as her implication. I will return, in spite of Doris, in spite of Downtown which is threatening either to dismiss me or transfer me because of what I said to their idiot graduation speaker. I doubt if they will do either. I'm not sure anyone else wants the job.

.

HUNTINGTON HOUSE is three stories of sooty gray stone and tired ivy, dusty windows that have to be opened outward by a hand crank, long dreary corridors of buckled linoleum, dark molding layered with varnish, cavernous bathrooms where the broken edges of little diamond tiles pinch the bare feet. The girls who live there are unmotivated, unreceptive, and critical. They are not eager to be taught and their primary verbal skill lies in the art of complaint.

"I *can't* do my paragraph. I don't *feel* well."

"Where don't you feel well, Orenthia? I'll ask Nurse Caulfield to send up some aspirins because I don't want you to miss the lesson on paragraphing."

"I'm not going to *write* any more paragraphs. I'm having false labor pains."

"How can you be having false labor pains? You're only in your fifth month."

"Well, I *said* false labor, didn't I!"

Huntington House is a maternity home. My students are under eighteen, unmarried, and pregnant. And I am tired of the joker who asks, "What can you teach pregnant teen-agers that they don't already know?"

I was hired to teach them English. I came to teach them Dylan Thomas and *Ethan Frome* and dependent clauses and punctuation and iambic pentameter. I wonder now if any of that is significant. There is too much that I cannot teach them, not yet, since there are things I don't understand myself, things concerned with the confusion of the heart. Not just theirs but mine. And although I came here by chance I will fight for this assignment, not only for what I can teach but because my own education is incomplete.

Before Mrs. Vanderveld made her sudden departure from Huntington House, I was in fact a member of the faculty of the most coveted school in the city, an architect's creation in glass and natural wood and stone, organically integrated into expensively verdant hills, and crammed with forty verbal adolescents to a class, five classes a day, and homeroom. Sometimes, with luck, thirty-five, but at least five of those were causing me anguish. Like Danny Ornstein, for instance, and his bare feet.

It doesn't make any difference to me if a student comes in with bare feet, but *bare feet* was the issue of the day. It was the mad bare-feet season and shoes were specifically required. I didn't make the rules. I only wanted to teach "The Love Song of J. Alfred Prufrock," and Danny Ornstein came slap-slapping into the room, maneuvering to catch my eye. I did not want a confrontation. I only wanted to teach *imagery and the sea.*

"Hot," he said as he stomped heavily in the vicinity of my desk. "I hate to be overdressed in hot weather."

"Where are you overdressed, Danny? If you sit down and stop weaving around you won't feel the heat."

"I admire you new teachers who wear flats. You don't need to stagger around on heels like some of the phonies in this place."

I kept my eyes on the class and away from his feet but I could smell them.

"I'd like to hit the imagery of 'Prufrock.' That we started yesterday as you remember? Four images, the sea, the hands, and what else?"

"Feet!" he called, sliding behind his desk and sticking his feet into the aisle.

"Where are there feet in 'Prufrock'?"

"Where he says 'Do I dare descend the stair with a bald spot in the middle of my hair.'"

"Where are the feet?"

"How could he descend the stair without feet?" He tattooed the floor with his heels.

"Danny," I said, "pick up your feet and get out. It's only eight-eighteen and it's already hot and I want to teach a lesson and you're being obstructionist. I'm not in the mood for social issues and I have four more classes and I'm tired of your feet. So please go soak your feet and your head in the men's room and let's get back to sea imagery!"

"Aha! So you have feelings! So you can be stirred to anger! Why don't you leave the sterile poetry of yesterday and throw yourself behind a valid cause. It's *tomorrow* that's important!"

"Feet? You want me to throw myself behind feet? And to-morrow I'm giving a test on the imagery of T. S. Eliot! So why does he make such an issue about water?"

"To wash Danny's feet!" yelled someone.

Unfortunately I didn't remember someone's name. It was the third week of the semester and I was facing almost two hundred students a day. And I was tired of it. It pressed in on me. I wanted to retire to where I could teach in a modicum of peace. To manageable numbers.

And I told as much to my friend J. over the phone that evening.

"I can't survive with these large classes. I have to get out."

"Again?" he asked.

"What do you mean 'again'? In that tone?"

"You've been teaching for three years and this is your third transfer. What are you running away from?"

"I'm not running. I'm searching for a comfortable space. I haven't found my dimension."

Let him make his insinuations.

"And if I am running, it's the 'madding crowd' I'm running from."

"Very literary," he said wryly. "But ask yourself — is it the truth?"

J. isn't Socrates. He doesn't teach school. I do.

And so when the time for transfer requests came around I desperately questioned my principal. Wasn't there a place where a teacher could teach to small groups, where a teacher could function in the way a teacher is supposed to function?

"If you have a little money in the bank start a small private school. Do you know that there are teachers who would give their eyeteeth to get this spot? If you want solitude, teach in a hospital. A nice quiet hospital room and a student in a body cast. Then you can teach one-to-one instead of one-to-forty. If you don't mind waiting for him to get out of surgery to deliver your lecture."

"One-to-one!" The thought intrigued me.

"I wasn't serious," he added. "You wouldn't like it."

"Why wouldn't I like it?"

"These are bedridden kids. I know you. You're better with bare feet than with twisted feet. It isn't your vocation."

Everyone thinks he knows my vocation. J. included.

"Look," I said, "all kids are handicapped these days. And all teachers." Sounds of slapping feet echoed in the hallway.

"Try it if you want to," he said reluctantly. "I guarantee you'll be back at the end of the year begging for forty healthy kids."

I filed my transfer request. Again. And the new semester found me happily independent with a briefcase of my favorite books and a stack of three-by-five cards, each stating the name and affliction of one homebound or hospitalized student. It was my responsibility to bring an assignment to each bedside, five to the working day. I was teaching and yet I was free. And my first group of students was not pitifully afflicted. Each was simply homebound with a case of temporary cyesis.

My first student was Elmira Watson. She greeted me at the door, her cyesis immediately evident, about the eighth month of it. She waited for me to enter, her hand resting on her stomach, the way women sometimes stand in the late months. She was fifteen and she needed to complete tenth-grade English. Through an open bedroom door I could see two other small children — her sister's baby, she explained, and her own small brother. Her mother had already left for work but the apartment was tidy and warm and a little pot of coffee intended for me rested on the stove. And Elmira was prepared, three little sharpened pencils like sentinels beside her notebook on the scrubbed kitchen table. "You want my homework?" she asked me.

I did. Proudly she handed me her paragraph, written in a large square hand.

> What is important to me. I do want a big weding with a white dress and a specal cake. I want the bridesmates in pink and a live band. But the baby is coming but it dont mater. My mother promised me the weding after.

She watched me make the corrections and mark the appropriate square in the grade book which was to her something magical. With pleasure she replaced the paper in her thick notebook of graded papers. She also explained that she was eager to have *nouns* because she didn't know *nouns* and once the baby came she might never get the chance to learn *nouns*. She delighted me. And her *cyesis* was no impediment to my teaching. I could not have asked for a more pleasureful hour. Let J. chew on that.

Unfortunately Velma Smith's house wasn't as tidy. Old newspapers and trash caught in the tall grasses of the front yard, and the skeleton of a Ford station wagon blocked the driveway. It must have died there and been stripped of all its usable parts until only the dull shell remained, wedged into the soil, eroded back to its base metal.

The house was too hot. The stove in the cluttered kitchen burned with the oven door open, and several mucusy children stood about fingering the books or climbing up on my lap to see me write. Parts of breakfast were still on the table.

I am very resilient but I can't stand heat. "Can we open the window please, Velma? We can't think without air."

She shrugged and opened one of the cracked windows.

"Can you turn off the stove?"

"The kids have colds," she protested.

"And do you think your mother might take care of the children while we have our lessons?"

I had tried holding the youngest on my lap but she dripped onto the grade book. I felt rotten as Velma shoved the protesting children into a bedroom and made a few swipes at clearing the table. I started my lecture on the importance of learning to communicate when I spotted a mouse. My response to mice is entirely involuntary. I lifted my feet to let it pass and I followed its voyage across the cluttered room with considerable alarm. When I returned to Velma her eyes were angry. And I was ashamed of my reaction. I mean you can't blame a girl for a mouse.

"So what!" she said defensively. "We got a cat!"

"I didn't mean to be critical," I explained to J. that evening on the phone. "I have a problem with mice."

"I told you it wasn't your vocation. You wanted a more personal encounter and mice come under the category of personal encounters."

"Mice are too personal."

"Do you know what you're looking for? Have you any idea what personal means? Personal isn't Molly Bloom's soliloquy or Hamlet's monologue. Hamlet talking to himself isn't personal. *Mice* are personal."

I had no intention of debating the point. But it was fortuitous that Mrs. Vanderveld's husband made his sudden decision to retire.

"Would you consider teaching in a maternity home?" begged my supervisor. "Mrs. Vanderveld up and left without notice for Tucson, Arizona. Her ungraded papers are still on her desk. Huntington House desperately needs an English teacher."

I would not admit it to J. but I desperately needed Huntington House.

"You're out of your mind!" said J. "If only one pregnant girl presses in, a whole school of them will stifle you."

"It was the mouse," I protested. "A maternity home would never tolerate mice. And the classes are small. And with all that time on their hands, they'll be delighted to do *Julius Caesar*."

I dragged J. across town to where Huntington House was located, a poor neighborhood in a forgotten corner of the city, with a certain quietness, a certain rural atmosphere that appealed to my spirit, a solitude that I think I had been searching for all along. Old frame houses with uneven porches, sloping and wind-dried but swept clean and made joyful with containers of flowers.

"I've never seen so many pregnant girls," marveled J. It did seem that way. Pregnant girls strolled the sidewalks in groups of twos or threes. Although there didn't seem many likely places to stroll. A drugstore, a self-service laundry, a tortilleria, a little coffee shop called Joe's Quicke Lunche, a very small supermarket, one dirty pet shop where the owner had jammed his puppies tightly into cages so that they climbed over each other's silken bodies to get to the bars with their damp noses. One little fat girl who seemed too young to be carrying a baby of her own leaned against the dirty glass to watch them.

"If you think this is the answer you're crazy," said J. over coffee in Joe's Quicke Lunche. "Why on earth would you want to teach in a maternity home? You'll miss the male response." J. has a certain egotism. "How are you going to teach 'Prufrock' to nervous, frightened pregnant girls? Just ask yourself, what can *you* teach pregnant girls that they don't already know?"

It was my intention on that optimistic afternoon to teach them composition and vocabulary and literary analysis. Everything that a smart teacher with a Master's in English can teach to high-school girls. I couldn't know then that I would also learn a lesson, a significant and vital lesson, from a sixteen-year-old girl without any judgment, without any logic, without any husband, with nothing as her text but an unborn baby named Heather.

Love's Labour's Lost

THE VW BUS was probably parked in the driveway when I arrived but I had not noticed it because as I climbed the steps I was worrying about Calpurnia.

The stone steps of Huntington House make a turn to the right before rising toward the double doors of the entry and I had paused at the turn to consider the problem of Caesar's wife. Calpurnia could bear no children. Caesar had specifically commanded Marc Antony, "Forget not in your speed, Antonius, to touch Calpurnia, for our elders say the barren, touched in this holy chase, shake off their sterile curse." Could I teach *Julius Caesar* without editing the script for students among whom not one was barren, not one was sterile? How could I explain Marc Antony running naked on the Feast of the Lupercal, trying to make Caesar's wife pregnant by hitting her with a goatskin whip? Could I discuss the phallic symbolism of the whip without getting too personal? Anyhow could I assume that pregnant girls knew more about sex than non-pregnant girls? Non-pregnant girls knew enough not to get pregnant.

If pregnant unwed girls read *Ethan Frome,* would there be a painful stirring of the ashes of old fires? Poor Ethan, longing with mute passion for his sweet young cousin and tied to his toothless old wife. Should I assume that pregnant girls suffered from unrequited love? Maybe they suffered from requited love. Maybe from love by force. Maybe from carelessness, with no love at all. Could I teach "How do I love thee? Let me count the ways"? What if someone cried? Bad enough *I* cried.

And so I didn't notice the girl who came up behind me until I heard a car door slam. A VW camping bus was backing out of the driveway and she had paused beside me on the turn to watch it go.

"God," she said in panic, "I blew it. I really blew it."

She stood for a moment, hovering before she continued, little wing bones of her shoulders clear against the thin tight shirt she wore, lithe girl with the tan of the outdoors still on her and a small obvious bulge where she had loosened the top buttons of her jeans. Which presented me with a further question. What does one say to a pregnant girl who carries a knapsack and wears her hair tied with an Indian band? She had spoken first. And she was in distress, her eyes fixed on the corner where the bus had disappeared. I could almost follow her fantasy the way I could follow her eyes — the bus would swing around, screech to a stop, she would fly down those steps again. But no car returned, and I could see her panic resolve itself into a bleak acceptance. She looked to me and shrugged her shoulders. And so I felt obliged to offer some words of solace. I searched for something appropriate, and literary.

"Don't worry," I said, in what I hoped was a warm tone. "The sun also *rises.*"

She glanced quizzically in my direction but she did not reply.

"The sun *sets,*" I explained, "but the sun also *rises.*"

"You're kidding," she said, and together we turned and climbed toward the entry. She dragged the knapsack of streaked canvas behind her, scraping the steps with it. She hesitated long enough to look over at me, to whip back the yellow hair with a horsetail flick. "Is that a cryptic saying or something?"

"It's the title of a novel by Ernest Hemingway."

"I never heard of it."

"Read it. The book gives meaning to the title."

I pulled the door open for her. She stood on the threshold, perplexed. "You actually mean that you want me to read a whole book so that I can figure out the title and get an answer to the little thing I just happened to say to you?"

"I suppose that's what I implied."

"Stupid," she said. "Really stupid."

She was absolutely right.

The door closed behind us. She dropped her knapsack in the entry, bent over it rummaging for something while I surveyed the bleak room. To the left a little alcove for visitors, a plastic sofa scarred by cigarette burns, some bland pastoral prints hanging crooked on enameled walls. Depressing. A door to the hallway through which I could see pregnant girls passing, none interested enough to give us more than a cursory glance. And to the right a glass door marked OFFICE. Three doors like three wishes or three feathers. Trinities have always fascinated me. I always get good paragraphs on trinities. Three blind mice, three little pigs. All that.

"Do you want a feel of my rock?" asked the Indian band. She held out what she had been searching for — a black rock, a beautiful oval stone which rested in the palm of her hand.

"Is that obsidian?" I asked her.

"Jesus, you're not supposed to label it. You're just supposed to feel it." She withdrew the stone, stood rubbing it against her cheek.

"Why not?" I asked her. "It seems to me that if you understand the history and the structure of the rock, you can enjoy it all the more."

Teaching is an art. Not confined to the classroom.

"Understand a *rock?*" She negated me with a toss of her head. "God!" She kicked off her sandals. Her bare feet were dusty. And familiar.

"Is that Sara?" called a welcoming voice. A tight brisk woman with a clipboard full of notes approached, hand outstretched to the girl from the VW bus. "It's about time. We expected you yesterday."

Sara shook the hand listlessly. "I wasn't in any rush."

"Cheer up," said the clipboard woman. "Huntington isn't so bad. You'll get along all right."

"Have I got any choice?" She kicked her knapsack into a sort of seat and sat on it, bony knees in the air and her head drooping between her shoulders.

The welcoming committee appraised her critically. "Sure you have choices. We always have choices."

"Thanks for the keen advice," she said. "I think I'm going to throw up."

The clipboard woman turned her appraising eyes on me. "Doris is waiting for you in the office. Vanderveld left us in a mess. I hope you don't have a husband with asthma." And then as an afterthought, "I hope you know what you're doing." And then as a mollification, "I'm Rodriguez. Office open any morning. Coffee's on in the kitchen. If you need it."

I happen to be a tea drinker. But I nodded my thanks and turned toward the office. I glanced about first, I remember, looking for an omen that would bode me well. I am not superstitious. Quite the contrary. But portents have a literary tradition and I searched for a symbol. A certain book on a table or a figure in a picture or a flower. I saw Currier and Ives prints, pots of ivy and cactus, a social worker making notes on a clipboard, and a weary teen-ager, sick to her stomach, empty with the loss of a VW bus, cleaning the dirt-filled nails of her toes. So I looked to my friend T. S. Eliot who advised me to "prepare a face to meet the faces that you meet." I prepared a smiling face and headed toward the office to find a head teacher named Doris.

A New Job and a Salty Baby

Doris is almost six feet tall, exceedingly thin, almost gaunt. Bending over a desk she is a question mark. Behind the desk a grandmotherly woman was watering her ivy with ice cubes. Doris uncurled to greet me. She rose taller and taller until her backbone was a rigid exclamation point.

Although I would never admit it to J., I find beginnings very difficult. Not the beginnings of things, the beginnings of people. The faces and the outstretched hands. But I had to suffer Doris and the opening amenities before I could enjoy the serenity of my new classroom. And the thought of that serenity gave me pleasure.

"This must be our new English teacher!" Her smile sharpened her cheekbones. She took my hand warmly, and did not release it.

"What happened to the old English teacher?" asked the elderly secretary.

"It was quite sudden," said Doris, hanging on to me with bony fingers. "She left for Tucson, Arizona, to live in a mobile home. We are *fortunate*" — she pressed my fingers to emphasize her sincerity — "to find a competent replacement on such short notice."

"Thank you," I responded. I wondered how to withdraw from her grasp without being ungracious.

Sara must have followed me because I caught a glimpse of her leaning against the doorjamb, watching our tableau with amusement.

"We are a family at Huntington House," said Doris earnestly. "We are deeply committed to our girls, as you well know, since you've worked long and hard on your Special Credential."

I didn't have a Special Credential, which I had been told was required for teaching handicapped but optional for "delicate" girls.

"Is my classroom upstairs?" I suggested. I looked hopefully toward the hall.

"Yes, upstairs." She pinned me with her eyes. "Or perhaps you are still working on it."

"No," I said as simply as I could, which at least effected the release of my hand. "If I could see my classroom," I asked again.

Doris was tenacious. "You mean you don't have it *yet*," she prompted.

Sara slouched against the doorpost, laughing silently.

"I mean I don't have it at all," I was forced to answer.

Doris stiffened at the disclosure. "Downtown will expect you to get it," she warned me. Like a parent to a sullen child. It was intolerable. And it was not serene.

"Hey!" A shout attracted our attention. To my relief. A wide-cheeked blousy girl, looking somewhat less than "delicate" in her nightclothes, stood awkwardly at the office door. Her feet in stretched-out slippers. Her hair still in fat curlers. "If any new girl comes in my room today I'm getting out of class!"

Miss Rodriguiz edged behind her. "Cookie, go upstairs and put on some clothes."

Cookie pulled her robe together over her belly with blunt nail-bitten fingers. "If a new girl comes into my room," she insisted, "I have to show her where to put her things in my closet!"

"She is not in your room, she's in Gail's. And where is Gail? I've looked all over the house for her. Do you mind taking Sara upstairs?"

"She's in the bathroom reading, that's where she is. Why can't Sara move in with me?" Cookie howled. "Then I can show her the closet space. If someone gets her shoes into my shoe corner I'll never get them out. I'll have somebody's shoes in my corner until I deliver!"

"Do you suppose I might go upstairs also?" I begged. "I'd like to put some notes up on the board."

Doris was stern, and single-minded. "Mrs. Vanderveld had a Special Credential. Downtown will ask you if you are working on it."

"Come on!" yelled Cookie from the stairway. Sara stayed and watched. The encounter was depressing me. My choices dwindled. And serenity was at the top of the stairs.

"If they ask me," I informed Doris, with my prepared face, my smiling face, "then I'll tell them I'm working on it."

She warmed with pleasure, froze, evaluating whether or not I was sincere, evidently decided that a teacher would never lie, contented herself. For the moment at least.

"Would one of you please announce schooltime," asked the old secretary. "Or the girls will go back to bed."

I reached over and took the little mike and called, "Schooltime!" My voice echoed through the old halls, into the walls, upstairs into some serene schoolroom with brown lacquered woodwork and silent corners and worn tables. I had arrived and I had announced myself. It was irrevocable. "Now will someone please direct me to my room."

Finally Sara started in the direction Cookie had taken and I followed close behind.

We were all trapped on the stairway by a small girl with a

large stomach who came slipping down in her haste, crowding around Cookie, around Sara, squeezing me face to face. The girl at the pet shop! Her sloppy bedroom slippers flapped against the steps. She made anxious, panting noises. Behind her descended a black girl, tight to bursting in a nightgown.

"Come back up here, dummy!" she called after the little girl.

"I won't, Wanda! Let me alone!" The little girl had lost a slipper, ran down the hall on one fat foot and one flopping shoe. Wanda squatted with effort to retrieve it. The pursuit ended at the end of the hall. A door slammed and locked. Wanda pounded it with the shoe.

"Open up, Baby! Come on out of there!"

"I won't!" came the pitiful reply.

Curious girls were gathering in the hallway. And I was caught in the crowd and it was pressing in. Miss Rodriguiz elbowed through to stand beside Wanda.

"Baby!" she called through the door. "What's the matter!"

"I'll tell you what's the matter!" announced a miniskirted nurse from the stair landing. "She bought a jar of pickles yesterday and she ate the whole jar and she's supposed to be off salt. And she's swollen and she's probably toxic. Do you hear me, Baby!" she called loud enough to reach the ears of the culprit.

"Leave me alone," came the pathetic reply.

"She's got to take a water shot and Dr. Lewin wants every girl up in the schoolroom right now for a talk. Baby, I'll wait for you in clinic!"

Schoolroom. My schoolroom! I pushed my way back to the office. "Is the doctor going to hold a meeting in my room? When will I meet with my first class?"

"He can't hold a meeting now," fretted Doris. "We've already called schooltime and this is Annabelle's day for the egg experiment."

"*What* egg experiment?" I asked frantically. "Do I have to share my schoolroom with the science teacher?"

"Annabelle has the basement schoolroom. She does her first egg this hour. If Dr. Lewin talks to the girls now she will miss her first egg!"

"Is today the eggs?" asked Miss Rodriguiz apologetically. "I didn't know that today was the eggs."

Over the loudspeaker the secretary's voice made the announcement, "All girls to the upstairs schoolroom for Dr. Lewin."

"Look," I asked, "at least let me go up and put some notes on the board while he's talking."

Annabelle came in carrying her egg box.

Doris is six feet tall and Annabelle weighs two hundred pounds. Annabelle easily lifted the large box marked BOARD OF EDUCATION — SCIENCE — EGGS onto the desk. "Good morning!" she boomed. "Is everybody ready for the big day?"

Nobody was. "Do you suppose you could delay your first egg until second period?" asked Miss Rodriguiz. "Dr. Lewin found another toxic girl and he's giving one of his talks."

"He can't!" roared Annabelle. "Let him talk after schooltime. The seniors see my first egg this period. And the little ones second. And the elevens third. If I miss my first egg the whole thing goes flat!"

"What egg experiment?" I asked.

"This is our new English teacher," explained Doris, as if I were the second problem of the day. She turned to me, distressed. "Did they tell you that you have to be flexible to teach in a maternity home?"

"I am flexible," I said. "I simply want to go to my room and put some notes on the board."

"*I'm* flexible," said Annabelle, "but my eggs aren't."

"I suggest that you go upstairs," said Doris finally, in that voice of hers, less a suggestion than a command. "Directly Dr. Lewin finishes, send the seniors down for the first egg. Do you understand?"

I was affronted by her question. "Yes, I understand. I speak English fluently."

"We only get the eggs once a year," complained Annabelle. "I can't tell you how much I look forward to this experiment," she said passionately. "Next to fertilizing the sea urchins this one is the best."

And I started up once more, hedged in by pregnant girls, a stranger in a strangely fertile land. Girls in curlers and bathrobes, still not dressed after breakfast. Smocks and pants and sandals and not much makeup. For whom, after all? Sara pressed beside me on the stairway.

"I hope you lie to Downtown," she laughed. "That's groovy."

"You think it's good to lie?" I asked her as we were pushed along the second-floor landing to the next flight up.

"Sure, if you lie for truth."

"I don't follow you," I said.

"Good. I'm glad you don't. You know what's the matter with you? You think too much. You ought to stop thinking and feel."

I bumped somebody's stomach. "Watch it," warned somebody.

I was rather amused by her swift judgments. "What leads you to think I don't feel?"

"I know your type. You don't feel. You just think you feel."

We had reached the third floor and we were pushed inside the schoolroom. Inside *my* schoolroom. With pregnant girls in every chair, on the edge of every table, fidgeting and shifting to make themselves comfortable while the doctor paced angrily, waiting for them to settle down. He strode to the blackboard, *my* blackboard, and in a strong hand he wrote OSMOSIS.

I edged next to Sara. "How does one know the difference between thinking one feels and actually feeling?"

She flicked her hair at me. "To begin with, *one* doesn't use stupid impersonal language, *does* one!" and she slipped through the crowd and went to stand at a window, her face pressed against the glass, looking for a VW bus. And I listened to Dr. Manfred Lewin as he addressed his girls.

You think you're funny, don't you. You think it's funny if a little girl goes out and gorges herself on salt and swells up like Tweedledum and puts herself in terrible danger!

Do you ever think of your kidneys?

And do you think that Baby is the only one? Four toxic girls this year! And after I gave Lucy in the kitchen strict orders for your diets, you run off to the drugstore and eat ice cream until you're waddling around and your poor kidneys trying to pump waste and having a bad time.

Did you ever hear of osmosis?

And what do you do to help your poor kidneys? Do you stop gorging yourself on hot fudge and whipped cream? No! You rush right out for potato chips and French fries and salted peanuts! I've seen you! And your heart, the poor hard-working heart, pumping away and all the tissues drawing water until you're as puffy as balloons! And toxic!

Until you stop this nonsense, I'm taking you all off salt. No more salt on the tables! No salted crackers! No bacon! No ham! Until everybody learns a little self-control! And I don't care if you can eat salt. Here at Huntington House you are your sister's keeper.

Okay?

The room was finally silent. Through the door came Wanda leading a reluctant Baby.

"How old are you, Baby?" asked the weary doctor.

"Thirteen and a half," she whimpered.

"Old enough to watch your salt, at least until you deliver?"

"I *hate* shots," she wept. "Belson sticks when she gives shots!"

"I told you Nurse Caulfield would give it, didn't I?"

She shook her head miserably, clasping her fat little hands together in anguish. He walked over to her, took her by the shoulder, led her to the door. Looking back at the girls he pleaded, "Watch the salt. Please?"

Finally I was able to step to the front of my classroom. "Will all seniors go downstairs for the egg experiment."

They began to drift off, those who weren't mine for that first hour, looking at me more out of curiosity than enthusiasm. I caught Sara as she was leaving.

"What's the difference between feeling and just thinking you feel?" I asked her again.

"Read *Siddhartha*," she advised me. "It's a novel by Hesse. Then think about the title. Maybe you'll make the connection." A swish of the hair and she was gone.

And I was alone, finally, with my first students at Huntington House. The door was closed. All was serene. Six tenth-graders slumped in disordered chairs, thinking about their kidneys.

"Will somebody please tell me," I asked them, "what is an egg experiment?"

The Egg Experiment

THE EGG EXPERIMENT
by
Mary Lou C.
Senior English
Per. 2
Topic Sentence and Support

We have to watch the egg experiment in Biology. In order
to see the fetuses (?) grow. Every day Mrs. Miller breaks
open this egg on a plate. At first it is nothing but a mess.
Then it turns into a chicken. Every day she breaks open another egg. Every day it has eyes or a beak or a heart of something that looks like a chicken. Then on the last day a wet
chicken begins to peck. It pecks alot. It pecks and pecks.
Then it breaks the shell. It looks terrible until the feathers
dry. Then it's cute. It's not Biology. It's an Act of God. I
am Catholic.

"Gail M. Advanced Composition."
Gail raised her hand but her eyes remained focused on the
book she was reading. I tried to make out the title. I was prob-
ably mistaken but it looked like Latin.
"Mary Lou C. Senior English."
Mary Lou lifted her hand in response but it went immediately

to her ornate hair, an art piece of braided coils. "I'm expecting my boyfriend from the Army. If he comes I'm leaving."

"Wanda S." She shifted her weight to accommodate the belly which seemed, to me at least, to be ripe. She acknowledged her name with a moan of discomfort. "How is the little toxic girl?" I asked her.

"Ask her yourself. She'll be here as soon as she gets her shot."

"How will she be here? This is *Senior* English."

"The nines are junior high school seniors," explained Gail from behind her book.

It could be managed. Yes. I would teach my generalizations to the common group and then divide them for individual assignments. One has to orchestrate a class. Organize it and blend it. Teaching is an art, not a job. That is what J. did not understand.

"Helen R. Business English."

Helen R. raised her hand and then continued the letter she was writing. It didn't look like business.

"Sara D. Advanced Composition." I was rather disappointed that she had entered without greeting me, that she had gone directly to a window and turned her attention to the street. "I know Sara already," I added.

"Do you?" she asked without turning.

Baby waddled in, face still red from weeping, still puffy about the eyelids. Another stout girl followed close behind. They were both ridiculously young to be carrying babies of their own. Tweedledum and Tweedledee. Like children at play they stood holding hands. In spite of the swelling bellies.

"Mary Catherine A. and . . ."

"Marlene H." said Baby, smiling a little-girl smile. "We share. Just give us the assignments. Mrs. Vanderveld let us work together."

"Laverne A." I didn't see any Laverne A. But I heard her.

A sort of gagging cough from the hallway and she came stagger-ing in, a hand to her stomach and a hand to her mouth, a face distorted with nausea. Laverne A. was Cookie.

"It was disgusting," she sputtered. "That sticky mess in the plate! I almost vomited!"

"It's supposed to teach you the fundamentals of pregnancy," said Gail from behind her book.

"Pregnancy!" gasped Cookie. "I'm not going to have a chicken!" She choked hysterically. "Does she think I'm going to have a chicken? What sort of F.O.B. does she think I had?"

I wasn't sure whether or not she was being vulgar. "What's F.O.B.?" I ventured.

"Father of baby," laughed Cookie. She had fallen heavily into a chair. "My F.O.B. wasn't a chicken! Cluck!" she cackled.

"You're a cluck," said Helen, without looking up from her let-ter.

"Cluck you," said Cookie.

I am partial to seniors. Seniors usually have the maturity to grasp abstract ideas. And they have more emotional stability. Here was my little group at last. Only seven. Nothing pressing in, except perhaps the discomfort of watching Sara at her win-dow post, her empty vigil. Just a fine old room with character, with history. English isn't taught well in glass and steel. It needs old brick and worn wood and little crooked corners and cracks. Especially cracks. And there was above all silence, and the sounds of doves which must have been roosting on the gray stone outside. Sara had found the doves already, had cranked open one of the windows, sat cooing at them.

I would describe this scene to J.

I would also describe Doris.

I erased OSMOSIS from the board and turned to face my stu-dents. It was with no small emotion that I spoke. "I know that you are all wondering about me."

"Cluck," said Cookie.

"About how I teach and what I teach. Well I want to tell you something about myself and I want you to feel absolutely free to ask questions."

Sara finally swung about to face me. "*Absolutely* free," she echoed. With a hint of derision.

All eyes were on me except Helen's. She bent over her letter. I try to be flexible in my teaching, but I really require the attention of the whole class when I'm lecturing.

"Helen, is that a business letter?"

She jumped when I called her name, smearing the ink. "Look what you did! My last piece of good paper!"

"Is that an assignment you're finishing for Mrs. Vanderveld?"

"Some assignment," laughed Cookie. "Cluck. Cluck."

Let it go. I was there and I had plans for these seniors. There would be time and space now to fire each imagination, to preside over each individual awakening. Especially for the two little fat ones. And so I spoke intensely because I believed in what I was saying.

"Every senior is old enough and mature enough to develop a personal philosophy, and what better way to develop a philosophy than to explore through your reading the philosophies of great writers."

"What is she talking about?" asked Helen.

"When I ask you to read a book I don't expect you to read for plot alone. Absolutely not. I want every senior in this room before she leaves this class to understand romanticism, realism, determinism, and existentialism."

Cookie gagged, shoved herself back from the table. "What are we going to do *that* stuff for? Why can't we do sentences the way we did with Mrs. Vanderveld? I don't want to do stories and that junk! I *did* stories already!"

"What kind of sentences?" I asked her.

"Just sentences. You know. Sentences!"

"But what do you do sentences *for?*"

She glared at me, making faces at my abysmal ignorance. "You do them for *credit!* That's what you do them for!"

"I mean what do you learn from doing sentences? How do they add to your store of knowledge?"

"Why do I have to add to my store of knowledge here?" she whined. "Why can't I just do my schoolwork and add to my store of knowledge later?"

"Cookie, why don't you shut up and let her explain," said Gail, closing her book finally.

"Cluck," said Cookie.

"And the junior high girls can work from fantasy to reality. From stories about ancient gods and goddesses and giants and heroes to teen tales about growing up and family conflicts."

"Why can't *we* do giants and heroes?" protested Cookie.

Baby and Marlene leaned back, contented and smiling, hands clasped on bellies, and I made a mental note to search for teen material relevant to conflicts and *their* growing families. "And from these we'll structure our discussions and find material for our paragraphs. Because when my students finish with me they really know the paragraph. That I guarantee you. "

"I believe you," said Sara. She shook off her sandals and wiggled her toes at me. "Did you ever read E. E. Cummings?"

"Certainly I've read E. E. Cummings."

" 'Life's not a paragraph,' " she quoted, " 'and death I think is no parenthesis.' Life is *not* a paragraph."

"Good. Right. But Sara, that statement is symbolic. As you'll discover when we study poetry. He didn't mean that phrase to have anything to do with composition."

"Who says he didn't? Why does your generation have to

interpret everything? Anyone who *feels* that sentence knows exactly what he means. As if philosophy has anything to do with living," she snorted. For the benefit of the class.

"Philosophy *is* living. Without philosophy you are adrift."

She dismissed me with a shrug, turning back to her window. "Your generation is as dense as pea soup."

I was amused by her attempts to provoke me. "My generation isn't so far from your generation."

"Regular or galactic years? Coo," she added, for the benefit of her doves.

"I'm not allowed to date until I'm fifteen," stated Baby, blinking through her still-swollen lids. "I never had a date with a boy." She and Marlene leaned together and giggled.

The disclosure took my attention from Sara's abrasive statement. "Never?" I asked, as casually as I could.

"I had a blow on the head," offered Marlene. "I had amnesia. I can't remember what happened for forty-eight hours."

"I can't go out with boys until I'm fifteen," reiterated Baby. "I wanted a Dalmatian puppy but my mother didn't let me because we have a beige rug. But she promised I can have one when I get home. I'm going to camp this summer."

"Everything for forty-eight hours is a blank," said Marlene. "I was riding my horse and I got hit in the head by a branch. He's white with a brown diamond on his nose."

But I cut her off. "I'm passing some three-by-five cards. I'd like you to list all the books you've read this year." I had come to teach English, not to do counseling. I was not equipped to do counseling.

"On one three-by-five card?" asked Gail. "Are you serious?"

"Take mine," offered Cookie.

From somewhere over the doorway came the old secretary's voice. "Family from Ontario coming through."

There was a loudspeaker in my room!

Cookie leaped away from the table, grabbed her purse, and without a word she fled.

"What's the matter with Cookie?" I cried, alarmed. "Did her water break?"

"She's only in her sixth," said Helen. "Water doesn't break in the sixth. Don't you know anything? When anyone comes through from your hometown you get to leave so they won't see you."

"We're anonymous," explained Gail. "We're also invisible. Cogito ergo sum. We think, therefore we are. But nobody here thinks very much."

"What's she talking about?" asked Helen. "She never talks regular."

I searched for the loudspeaker. "Let's get rid of this. I'm sure we can hear the announcements from the hall."

"We have to have a loudspeaker," wailed Baby. "We have to know if it's our turn for clinic."

"You get called out of class for clinic? In the middle of a lesson?"

Our door was pushed open by a hesitant hand, admitting a frightened girl. And her mother, probably, an anxious thin-faced woman who held her daughter's hand. And Miss Rodriguiz and her clipboard standing protectively by.

"This is the classroom," Miss Rodriguiz explained, "where the girls continue their regular schoolwork until they deliver."

The girl let her eyes drift nervously about the room. Suddenly she saw Helen, her fear gave way to a smile of recognition. She waved. Helen waved back. And the door closed. The tourists left for other places.

"Do people always walk in like that?" I asked. "Without notice?"

"You're so terribly hung up on privacy," said Sara from her window. "Your type always is."

"She's from my school," explained Helen. "I heard she was coming."

"Then why didn't you leave with Cookie?"

"What do I care who sees me? I only came here because my probation officer made me. They can publish my picture in the newspaper for all I care. And Cookie comes from San Diego."

"Then why did she run out?"

"She was worried about her closet."

"But she's not permitted to leave class to see about closets."

"What difference does it make if she leaves or if I leave?" Sara was laughing quietly.

"Is it okay if I double up my work?" asked Wanda. "I want to get full credit before I go over."

"Over where?" I asked.

"To the hospital," explained Gail. "Euphemism. *"Go over* means letting your uterus expel the child and having an episiotomy and getting stitched up and all that. Simplification. Like chickens and eggs."

"Wouldn't it be easier to complete your work in your own school after you deliver?"

Wanda's thin shoulders slumped against the back of the chair, her taut stomach almost at level with the table. "With the baby crying and the diapers?"

She surprised me. I had naturally supposed that a girl who had given up her name for anonymity would give her baby out for adoption. "I see. Then you're keeping your baby and you want to complete the semester's work before you go over."

"Yes. I am keeping my baby." That, followed by a cold stare, a tightness of the lips. And we all sat in silence while I tried to figure out what inappropriate statement I had made. Wanda pushed back from the table, took her notebook and purse, and stalked out.

A few more and I would be teaching the doves out on the ledge.

And they all sat watching me, waiting for what came next. Baby pulled a strand of lank hair, her puffy features kittenish and imploring. Marlene edged close to her. Gail reopened her book. Helen went back to her letter. Mary Lou opened a movie magazine which she had stashed inside her notebook. Sara kept her window vigil, but she spoke to me. "She's keeping her baby because she's very proud and she loves her baby."

"I see."

"Nobody in your generation sees. You're blind. *One* doesn't give up *one's* baby easily, *does* one! Just let anybody try to take mine."

"Who wants to?" asked Gail.

Sara brushed the question aside, twisted restlessly at the window. "Anyone in this place have a guitar?" she asked, scratching the screen at the unseen birds. Nobody responded. And then without introduction and without self-consciousness and without a guitar she began to sing. Softly, in a thin high voice.

> *Come all ye fair and tender maids*
> *Who languish in your prime*
> *Beware, beware, make your gardens fair*
> *Let no man steal your thyme . . .*

"Is that the song of the herbs?" asked Gail in admiration. "I think it's Elizabethan."

> *And when your thyme is past and gone*
> *They'll care no more for you*
> *And all your lovely flowers there*
> *Covered over with rue . . .*

". . . *rue,*" she sang once more in that thin liquid voice.

"Beautiful," I said. I was touched by her song. "That's *exactly* what I want from this class. I invite you all to be spontaneous."

Sara released a whoop of laughter. "Do you *know* what spontaneous means? Have you ever thrown off your clothes and jumped into an icy waterfall with a bunch of strangers? Did you ever squish your toes in the mud after a winter rain?"

The others listened eagerly for my reply. I wasn't about to discuss my spontaneous activities with a sixteen-year-old whose concept of spontaneity was mud pies.

"I think Ophelia drowned herself because she was pregnant," said Gail.

That was more like it. I had never bathed naked in ice water, but literary sleuthing was my favorite sport. "Marvelous," I said. "What lines do you use to support your theory? Does Hamlet suspect? Is that part of his melancholy?"

"Not by Hamlet. By her brother Laertes. The whole thing is incestuous. You have to read between the lines."

"I don't know what *anyone* is talking about," said Helen.

"*We* are the gardens," said Sara wistfully.

"Nostra culpa," said Gail. "We didn't keep our gates closed."

"What fun is a closed gate?" asked Sara.

And the hour was over. They picked up their notebooks and purses and without any assignment they all slowly filed out. No one bothered to acknowledge our new relationship with any comment, except for Sara. She paused at my desk, leaned over my shoulder, speaking through a curtain of heavy yellow hair. "Baby only got pregnant to get the puppy," she laughed. "You know that, don't you."

She turned and they were gone.

"Okay," said J. that evening over the phone. "Let's have it."

"What?"

"The usual description of the freaks you work with. Which one is at least five feet eleven?"

"Doris. Six feet if she's an inch. I have more to say about Doris."

"Of course you have. And which one weighs one eighty in her gym clothes?"

"Annabelle. Two hundred. And solid."

"And who has the vocabulary of a four-year-old?"

"Are you being sarcastic?"

"Not at all. What's the catch this time?"

"There's no catch. They're just one happy family."

"And when are you leaving home?"

"Did you know that F.O.B. means father of baby?"

"Oh?"

"Can you believe that we have a pregnant thirteen-year-old?"

"I'm happy that someone is getting pleasure out of youth." He hesitated, less acerbic. "Are you staying with this job?"

"Did you ever consider that Ophelia might have drowned herself because she was pregnant?"

"By Hamlet? Not that girl. She's like women I know. She would never do anything that joyful and unpremeditated."

"By Laertes. You have to read between the lines. Do you know the best way for kids to escape the overcrowded city classrooms?"

"I'm afraid to ask."

"Just get pregnant."

"When it presses in," said J., "when it starts pressing in again, you might remember that."

The Seventeen Perversions of Love

I STARTED with Ethan Frome because he had never failed me. The anguish of his impossible love. The impotence of his passion for Mattie. I don't read the scenes aloud because I cry. And so it came as a surprise to me that Ethan's horrible accident, his aborted suicide, and the near death of his lover did not interest the girls of Huntington House as much as the details of someone's constipation. The torture of Ethan's lying in bed beside the toothless old wife while his lover moved softly, inaccessible in the next room, could not compare with the fact that somebody's uterus had grown a centimeter larger. And when they sat staring at me with pencils poised, they were actually listening to something visceral. If I asked a question they sat blankly waiting for their babies to move. They giggled. They were sleepy. They were slightly nauseated. They were cramped or nervous or bilious. But they were not interested.

I had failed to stir them out of that lethargy. The thought disturbed me as I climbed the stone steps. Sara caught me as I entered.

"Okay if I wear shorts to class?" Tidy shorts, covered by an overblouse of tie-dyed material, evidently of her own design. Perhaps she had dyed it with the stains of wild berries beside an icy waterfall. With her bare feet in the spontaneous mud.

"Did you finish the conclusion of *Ethan Frome*?"

"God, I wish you'd never given me that book!" Her face contorted with displeasure. "It was pitiful."

Sara at least was moved. Here was my starting place. This foolish Sara.

"They were crazy, the two of them! Just sitting in that crummy kitchen and wanting to make love and they didn't have the guts. It's stupid. Just because he felt guilty about his toothless, selfish old wife. And even if he did take a chance and do it, he couldn't have made proper love. You can't really love if you feel guilty. You know that." The statement caught in her voice. Whatever association it made she quickly shrugged off. "I'll never understand your generation."

"Sara, it's not *my* generation. And you've missed the point. You can observe how other people deal with the passions of their lives. Or you can empathize with their pain. Or if you don't like the way they act you can pass judgment on how the author drew his characters. But you can't pass judgment on the characters as if they created themselves. Do you understand what I mean?"

"Who says I can't? Teachers are ridiculous. The last person anyone should learn from is a teacher. If your generation had its way you'd give us a script of exactly what to think about when we're sitting on the can. And what do you know about passion?" She mocked me with judgmental eyes.

I was not going to be provoked by a sixteen-year-old mud-pie maker.

"So it's okay if I wear shorts?"

As far as I was concerned. It was not the costume that disturbed me but the girl. "That's a groovy blouse," I told her.

"People your age shouldn't use *groovy*. It's artificial."

"Sara, I'm just not that old."

"Teachers are born old. Teachers think love comes under L in the card catalog. Have you ever made love in broad daylight just because the water was green and the surf was white and the little birds pecking in the wet sand made you hot and crazy?"

I searched through my experience for an appropriate answer.

She smiled cleverly. "Doris absolutely forbids shorts in class. You know that, don't you." She flicked her hair and walked off.

"Did you say she could wear shorts to class?" asked the old secretary as I entered the office. "Doris absolutely forbids shorts in the classroom."

I had more serious problems than shorts and love in the tide pools. My English 10's were sleeping through *Julius Caesar*. I could wake them up for Portia because she stabbed herself in the leg for love. And they remembered that poor Calpurnia got whacked with Antony's whip. But Cassius was impossible. If the girls were going to get heartburn they would get it for Cassius.

"By the way," added the secretary, "Annabelle is stuck with a flat on the freeway. She may not be in until very late. She said she phoned for a substitute to take her classes."

"Schooltime!" I called through the little mike. I was sorry she'd called for a sub. If they had some free time they might be tempted to finish my assignments. Which they rarely did. On my way upstairs I noticed three other girls wearing shorts.

I spent the better part of the first hour trying to teach why Cassius was lean and hungry. I wanted them to feel a hunger for something that was not food. Power, for instance. Or fame. Cassius was ambitious. They were lethargic. He was conniving. They were apathetic. And I was jealous of Annabelle's sea urchins which were so beautifully relevant. The hour was a loss. I could not move the girls.

Cookie could. She burst into the room, leaning limply against the bookcase, signaling that she had to take in air before she could speak.

"We have a sub," she sputtered. "He's a man," she panted. "He looks like Steve McQueen," she moaned. "He has sandy hair! He has blue eyes! I'm dying!"

Golda, who had been dozing for the better part of the hour, was already on her feet.

"Where are you going?" I asked her.

"I have to turn in my homework."

"You don't have science until second period. You can turn it in then."

"But I'm supposed to turn it in at the beginning of the day or I won't get credit."

"She's supposed to turn it in at the beginning of the day," corroborated Cookie, "or she won't get credit."

"But Mrs. Miller isn't even here. She's stuck on the freeway with a flat. So how can Golda get credit?"

Cookie was already on her way back to the stairway. Golda slammed her books on the table. And I tried to return to Cassius. "What does it mean to have a lean and hungry look? Do you know anybody who looks lean and hungry?"

"Nobody in *this* place," said Golda. "Why do we have to do this dead-type work when there's something interesting happening?"

"It's only a substitute. You'll see him second period."

She didn't hear me. Nobody heard me. They were staring, dumfounded, at the doorway where *he* stood, his eyes fastened on *them*. A poet. The eyes of a dreamer. Hair wild and free. An old pullover sweater. As a matter of fact he didn't look anything like Steve McQueen. He was Michelangelo's David. A perplexed smile of dramatic intensity. Eyes questioning and open and frank. I had a momentary pang of jealousy for anyone who could make the girls come alive so quickly. Only momentary. Because my annoyance was tempered by his beauty.

"Unbelievable," he muttered. "Where am I?"

"This is English 10," I explained. "Did you find the sea urchins?"

"I had two hospital patients last week." His voice was resonant and as he spoke he kept his eyes fastened on the girls. Terribly clear blue eyes. "To pick up some bread while I'm writing my play. So when I got the call I naturally thought that this was a hospital."

The girls tittered. They had already pushed back their hair, tied their ribbons, drawn their knees together, pulled down their skirts and shorts. Their voices had risen in pitch. They blushed. They fluttered eyelashes and fingers. They were in love.

"Beautiful," he exclaimed to the world in general. "Pregnant women are so blasted beautiful. Like ripe fruit." He moved his hands in ripe-fruity motions.

Inadvertently I found my hand on my own flat belly.

"What *is* this place?" he asked in joyous confusion. "The secretary wouldn't tell me a damn thing."

"This is a maternity home. I don't think we're supposed to have male subs."

The implications of maternity home came to him slowly. His mouth moved in sympathy. His eyes softened to them. "Isn't anybody in this place *married?*"

They shook their heads.

The audacity of his question surprised me. I would have considered such a statement an intrusion into the privacy of their griefs. But nobody seemed to mind it.

"You *poor kids!*" He spoke with infinite compassion. He could have opened his arms and swept them all to his bosom. He leaned toward them as he spoke. "And look what they've done to you," he said bitterly. "Hidden you in this hole when they should be painting you and throwing flowers at your feet."

"Yes!" cried Golda. "Yes!"

"Do you all have science? Will I see you all later?"

"Yes!" they cried. Certainly untrue.

"Later then," he promised them. He turned and descended. Like Orpheus. The whole class rose to follow.

"Relax. You'll see him later. He's only a sub."

They stared at my madness. I *was* mad. I could easily have followed him myself. They slumped down in their chairs, discontented and restless. Cassius was a dead loss. The class mind was gone to men. He had stirred dormant emotions, wounds, dreams, disappointments, memories of love. I could read their faces easier than I could read their essays. A damp eye was touched by Kleenex. Someone sighed.

They had left me for a secret place. How could I offer them iambic pentameter when they were dreaming of some lost boy's loving hand? Or some brutal hand that was already romanticized by time and distance. Foolish girls. Deserted perhaps by the same sort of man who had just descended, who had cast his love like a net, trapped them, and disappeared. Foolish. All of them.

The rest of the hour passed in silence. They watched the clock for a signal of their release to him. So that they were jolted by the reality of him when he suddenly reappeared. They yearned toward him as he leaned over my desk.

"I'm a mistake," he said regretfully, taking my arm in his warm fingers as he spoke. "They called me back. I'm supposed to be at the General Hospital."

Cookie must have climbed up behind him. "No," she huffed. "You're *not* a mistake."

Sara followed Cookie, brushing her hair from her eyes. Wet from crying. She held some silent communication with the sub.

"He'll come back, kid," he said gently. "Don't stop loving."

She shook her head. "I couldn't. I wouldn't know how."

He released my arm. "Look," he said to me, with less intimacy than his eyes had shown Sara, "pick up my assignments, will you? They might interest someone in this mausoleum."

He patted Cookie's cheek as he passed her. "I'll never forget you, Cookie." He smiled at them all. And he was gone.

"He'll never forget me," said Cookie, awe-stricken, fingering the place on her cheek with nail-bitten fingers.

"I love him," said Sara.

When had he found time in his wooing to give them assignments? I could still feel the pressure of his fingers on my arm. Perhaps they had come to Huntington House because of warm fingers like his. So easily trusted. So quickly released.

And Sara stood beguiled and tearful. "You can't mean love," I chided her. "You were intrigued by him or you liked him. But you can't mean love, not on such short acquaintance. Not with any sort of depth or meaning."

"You and your labels. You should have been a grocery clerk, not a teacher. If your heart is open you can love a stranger. You wouldn't know about that. Your heart is shut. Think about it."

The rest of the day was impossible. Three girls climbed upstairs to protest his departure. "Don't we get his assignment?" They hugged their bellies — flushed, bloated, discontent.

Gullible. Their own fault that they were stuck at Huntington House. They rose so quickly to the bait of a gentle voice.

.

I mentioned the sub briefly, in passing, to J. over the phone that evening. "In half an hour he managed to throw the whole house into turmoil."

"What turmoil?" he laughed. "He brought them a half hour of happiness. That's more than you did with your whole *Ethan Frome.*"

I should have known better than to bring it up at all. "A half hour of happiness and nine months with a big belly."

"Happiness is a scarce commodity," he said. "Not involved with weights and measures."

"You're not funny," I told him. Annoyed.

"I wasn't *being* funny," he responded.

On some subjects the man is absolutely predictable. And I was in no mood to debate him.

.

I expected to find them sullen the next morning, angry at the loss of him. But every girl bent a head over an assignment sheet, pored over dictionaries and encyclopedias they had lugged over from the bookshelves for the first time that semester, sat contented, actually giggling as they worked. His assignment! And they were totally involved. Even my seniors!

Not every girl. Gail bent over a book of poetry. I couldn't see the title. And Sara pressed her cheek against the cool glass of her window, eyes closed in pain.

I watched the rest of them in astonishment and dismay. And I welcomed the intrusion of Nurse Caulfield.

"Hey," she asked, "what's troilism?" She held his assignment sheet.

"I don't know anything about science. Ask Annabelle. They certainly like it better than English. What is it, something glandular?"

"I got onanism and sadism and sodomy, but I never even heard of troilism."

I asked to see the sub's assignment. Flurries of laughter drifted about as we conferred. Actually it was a vocabulary lesson. "Identify the following perversions." There were seventeen.

Audacious. Like the questions he asked them. Impertinent. But, I had to admit that my class was awake. Not only awake but involved. I would even say *engrossed*.

Annabelle puffed in, settled her bulk in a chair. She held

up a list of her own. "What sort of a crazy sub did I have yesterday? What is this junk?"

"Do you usually get this much enthusiasm out of your science
assignments?" I asked her.

"Are you joking?"

It may have been junk and it may have been perverse, but
they liked it and dictionary pages were being turned at last, and
encyclopedias were being removed from their dusty cupboards.
Only Sara's bitter glance in my direction marred what appeared
to be a happy classroom.

Give the devil his due. A teacher learns where she can. De-
fining perversions had its value. Maybe I should have been
making little literary puzzles for them. Or word games. In fact
I had forgotten how much I loved puzzles when I was younger.
I got sixteen of the perversions without trouble. And Nurse
Caulfield, with her science training, only had twelve. Annabelle
didn't even have ten. Our little conspirators' table compared
notes.

"Most of the girls didn't even know what perversions *were*,"
whispered Nurse Caulfield as she filled in her blanks. "Some of
these girls are terribly naïve. They claim that they got caught
in the passion of the moment. I even had one virgin who insisted
the sperm got close and climbed up."

"It could happen," whispered Annabelle. "Just watch those
active little buggers under the microscope."

Cookie crowded into our circle. "What's onanism?" she asked.

"It's where he spreads his seed on the ground," said Nurse
Caulfield.

"What's so perverted about farming?" asked Cookie. "Hardly
any perversions are in the dictionary. They have lousy dictionaries in this place. How are you supposed to learn anything with
these dictionaries?"

"I don't think the Catholics would like this," called Mary Lou. "What's troilism?"

Actually nobody knew. It was a linguistic treasure hunt and I was delighted with it myself. We tried to discover the root. "Has it anything to do with Troy?" asked Nurse Caulfield. "Did they do perverted things in Troy?"

I have a Master's in English but I am not very strong in Ancient History. "I think they had perversions in Rome but I don't know about Troy. Who has a degree in History?"

"Doris," said Annabelle. "But don't ask her. She thinks kissing her husband on the public street is a perversion."

"I think Troy was more martial than perverted," I said. "How about the French *troi?*"

"Hasn't got an *l*," said Annabelle. "Wouldn't it be *troi-ism?*"

"Not at all," I added, supported by a couple of lessons in linguistics. "I-i is not a permissible sequence. So you tend to provide a consonant. Like people in Brooklyn who say bananersplit."

"Could it be related to *toil?*" asked Nurse Caulfield. "Where you have to work hard at it?"

"Then it would be *toilism*," laughed Gail from behind her book. I saw now what she was reading — *Troilus and Cressida.* Of course. *Good* for Gail. Troilus, troilism. She had the makings of a first-rate literary sleuth.

"I think her uncle betrayed her," said Gail. "It may have to do with a voyeur. I have to research it because I've forgotten my French."

"What's a voyeur?" asked Cookie.

"It's when someone's watching," said Nurse Caulfield.

"Oh I'd hate that," exclaimed Cookie. "The least a person ought to have is privacy."

"You're CRAZY!" screamed Sara, jolting us all with her strident cry. "You know that, don't you!" She beat both fists on the table. "You're fantastic! Your whole generation is nuts! You don't even recognize a joke when you see one!"

"I don't see any humor in perversions," said Annabelle.

"What I really object to," said Nurse Caulfield, "is his calling masturbation a perversion. That's pretty old-fashioned."

"My list says perversions *so-called* by a sick society," said Annabelle.

"You're all sick," said Sara bitterly. "You're sick in the head. You see words and you don't see what's behind them. Can't you see that these are all society's crummy labels for love? Does anyone in this place know what love is?"

"I know what love *does*," said Nurse Caulfield. "I see every one of you up in the stirrups in clinic."

"I said *love*, not sex!"

"Well, I understand sex," said Annabelle. "I see it happening right under my microscope. But I admit I don't see much love among the urchins."

"God," moaned Sara, "I've got to get out of here before *I* get perverted. You know what perversion is, don't you? It's your loveless world. And what about you!" she accused, pointing her finger at me. "You and your Ethan Frome. Love is so natural and beautiful and your generation has perverted it seventeen times seventeen."

I was moved by the sincerity of her statement but I had to evaluate it in terms of sex in the surf and a missing VW bus.

"Sara, if your definition of love is different from ours why don't you write an essay. Define love in your terms. Give some examples, so that we can understand exactly what you mean."

"Pitiful," she said, clutching her stomach. "They don't understand a word I'm saying. I'm in a loony house. If I stay here any longer I'll go out of my mind." She sobbed one dramatic sob and ran from the room.

Gail closed her book, disturbed by the outburst, and followed Sara. The rest in their embarrassment turned back to their assignments. My assignments. And they stared glumly at the pages.

"Don't let it get to you," Nurse Caulfield consoled me. "Have you noticed how big she's getting? I think she's just realized that it's not going to disappear."

I had to accept her evaluation. But Sara's constant accusations were beginning to press in. Why me? Why always me?

Nobody turned in the sub's assignment. But his absence was palpable. The apathy returned. And the perversions lingered on.

"What's sodomy?" asked Cookie a couple of days later.

I must not have heard her the first time because I was watching Sara, depressed after her explosion, sitting every class hour at the window, vaguely running a finger over the dusty glass.

"Hey!" yelled Cookie. "What's sodomy? Don't you hear me?"

"It pertains to animals," I answered, as simply as I could.

"I *still* don't understand what's so perverted about farming."

Socks, Smocks, and Buskins

THEY FASCINATE ME," I told J. over the phone. "But Sara is right. I don't understand them. Either they sit and brood or they flail about uselessly when they could be putting their energies into something productive."

"What do you *mean* productive! Those kids are creating life. What are you creating?" he asked testily.

"Their bodies are creating life. But their heads are still unoccupied. That's why I'm starting a theater group."

"Are you serious?" he asked. "With pregnant actresses?"

"Exactly." Actually, I was excited about the whole idea. "When their bodies are all bottled up, they take cathartics, don't they? I certainly hear enough about that. But what do they do when their spirits are bottled up? Nothing but sit and bite their nails. If they can only empathize with something outside their own little problems they might purge their troubled spirits. Like the Greeks. A catharsis of the spirit."

"Then don't put on plays with them. Invite one home for the weekend. Set your hair together and have some girl talk. See what it feels like to be fifteen and knocked up."

"You don't understand what I'm telling you. I'm not a group therapist. I'm an English teacher."

"Naturally," he said. "I should have known."

"And nobody wants to read. Except for Gail, and she's submerged in the Complete Shakespeare and she rarely comes to the surface. So I want them to do some short scenes. You just wait and see if I don't get some real enthusiasm out of them. And teach them something about empathy and catharsis."

"What do you know about empathy anyhow?" asked J. Not without a tinge of bitterness. The man is so emotional. "Do you ever empathize with me?"

"What do you think of *The Glass Menagerie?* Do you remember the play about the crippled girl and her domineering mother? They ought to empathize with that."

"Who do *you* empathize with? The girl who doesn't have the courage to cut loose and take love or the manipulating woman who messes up everyone's life?"

"Whom."

"Whom what?"

"*Whom* do I empathize with. Not *who*. It's the objective case."

"So are you," he said, before he hung up.

I could hardly wait to get started. I mean I had been feeling my way, after all. Learning the limitations of my environment. Now I was ready to swing free. So to speak.

"Don't you think it unbecoming to have pregnant girls in a play?" asked Doris, alarmed as usual. "We've never had a play at Huntington House."

"Let's try one and see what happens."

"You'll be careful of your choice of materials," she warned.

"I'm a professional teacher, Doris. Trust me."

There was nothing in her manner to indicate that she did.

In spite of Doris I began to cast my first production. And there seemed to be no lack of talent. Cookie had been giving a performance of her own every morning. It was a while yet until summer but an unexpected blanket of heat was provoking tempers which at best were volatile. Cookie, growing larger every day, dreamed up an object for her discontent, the big "house next door."

"They should have this big house next door and they should put all the F.O.B.'s in this big house!"

"S.O.B.'s would be better," said Helen.

"And they should hang weights on them every week, each time heavier, and they should eat the same slop that Lucy cooks."

"They should have barbed wire," added Helen, "and they should only get out on special passes."

"And they should have to get shots every morning," said Cookie, "with this big rusty needle . . ."

"*Belson* should give the shots," added Baby.

"And they should have *homework* to do!" said Cookie. Which wounded me because my assignments were both valid and relevant. As relevant as possible under the circumstances.

"Right next door," said Sara wistfully from her window post, "with a park and some trees and an underground stream and a tunnel that stretches into another world."

"A tunnel," agreed Cookie, relenting a little, "between the houses so we could visit." She looked down at her stomach in which her odd-shaped embryo was growing, straight out in front of her like a little sloping table. "Bastards," she said. Not bitterly. Just a commentary.

"So I think it's about time for our drama unit," I suggested, by way of an opening.

"Not another unit!" wailed Cookie. "Why can't we just rest awhile?"

"Because there's no unit in resting," said Sara. "There's no label for it."

"I thought we might start a little theater group and put on some plays of our own."

I waited for reponse. Hoping. Yes. They did. They looked alert. They were listening.

"Not a whole play necessarily. But some scenes. And the play I had in mind concerns a poor crippled girl and her domineering mother."

"Let me be the crippled girl!" begged Cookie. "I can do it. I'm handicapped too."

I was delighted with the immediate response, but I didn't realize that Cookie was handicapped. I had never noticed a limp or any other motor problem.

"I'm sorry, Cookie. Where are you handicapped?"

"It says in my records. You can see for yourself."

"Cookie, that's a technicality. You're not handicapped. You're actually delicate."

"She's more handicapped than delicate," laughed Gail. "Give her the part."

"And what about the rest of you?" I addressed myself to Sara who sat slumped against her window, no longer looking out, just inward and listless.

"Play-act," she said bitterly. "That's as close as your generation comes to living. Then the curtain comes down and you crawl back into your coffin."

"Acting can be very therapeutic," said Gail. "But can't we do something more mature than *Glass Menagerie*. Albee has some fairly interesting one-acters. Like *The Zoo Story*."

Marvelous. "That's a good choice." I told her. "A good play about conformity and the individual."

"Only if you read on the surface," said Gail. "It's a religious allegory. I'll play the weak and ineffectual mankind provoked by God into a Crucifixion if Sara will play God."

"Watch it," said Mary Lou. "I'm Catholic."

"What else is there to do," said Sara, dropping her arms dead against her sides and leaning her head back into space. "I might as well. If I don't get out of here soon I'll die in this hole."

"And what about the scenery?" I threw that one out casually.

"We will!" screamed Baby and Marlene. "We'll make it!"

"And we ought to have some programs typed," I said in Helen's direction.

She looked up from a letter she was writing. "Can I get extra credit?" she asked suspiciously.

"And someone will have to introduce the scenes. What about Mary Lou?"

"All right," she said reluctantly, "but if my boyfriend comes I'll have to leave." Which seemed a safe choice. Because in all the weeks I had been there I had seen no soldier on the premises.

"And where's Wanda? Why isn't she in class today?"

"Didn't you see the delivery board?" asked Helen. "She went over. She's so lucky." Her voice was filled with envy.

"Why can't it be me?" moaned Cookie.

"My mother promised me the puppy after," said a worried Baby. "I hope she won't go back on her promise."

There was a pall over my enthusiastic little theater group. Sara cast me a cutting glance, signaling the end of the first meeting of The Huntington Players.

But the play was on! The downstairs living room became our rehearsal hall and theater. The fireplace wall would hold the scenery and the potted schefflera would make a fine park for Gail's zoo.

"But," cautioned Doris, who stood with Miss Rodriguiz as I paced off the living room, "you may *not* put up anything with thumbtacks. Use Scotch Tape if you must. Carefully. But no thumbtacks. We cannot upset the housekeeper."

"Great!" said Miss Rodriguiz, making notes on her clipboard.

"I can only hope you take into consideration the problems of pregnant actresses."

"We don't expect to do any leaping around. So I don't expect any problems. In any case solving problems is part of the educational experience."

"Whose?" she asked. "Theirs or yours?"

I was well aware of the reason for her comment. Territoriality. She wanted their problems and their egos. That was her territory. The way Nurse Caulfield wanted their arms, the small vein for her needle. The way Doris wanted their credits for her school records. But I wanted their open and responsive minds.

"Shall I leave out the dirty parts when I type the scripts?" asked Helen.

"There are no dirty parts in good literature," I explained to her. "Only realistic details."

"I'll leave the dirty places blank," she said. "You write them in. I'm in enough trouble already."

"If the Catholics don't pass it," said Mary Lou, "I'm not going to introduce it. And if my boyfriend comes I'm leaving."

Our first real rehearsal took place on an airless day. Sara squatted on her knees on the overstuffed velvet sofa, pulling aside dust-filled velour curtains to catch a glimpse of the street outside. The living room bordered the driveway where the VW bus had been parked on that first day. I know what she was thinking as she watched that empty spot where no bus stood. At least I thought I did. Gail watched also, pulling nervously at the rubber knife which I had provided as a prop for the death scene. Self-pity and nail-biting. I had started my theater group none too soon.

"Let's begin with Gail's *Zoo Story*. Remember this is symbolism. The victim, that's Sara, offers the killer a knife and sacrifices herself, so it's not a real murder."

"Nothing is real to you," muttered Sara from the folds of the curtains. "I can't get the window up." The room was airless. Cookie fanned her heavy breasts with a script. Sara bounced off the sofa. "Okay," she said directly to me, "kill me. You might as well. I'm suffocating in this place."

The whole group gathered to watch. Gail was relieved to see Sara's response.

"The most important symbol is the stabbing," said Gail, "because the act of killing means rebirth."

"Try it," I suggested. "We'll see how it goes."

There they were. My alert participating group. The way I had imagined them. I knew that sooner or later I would hit the right unit. It was a matter of trial and error. That's the way a teacher learns.

"Where shall I stab her?" asked Gail. "She's getting pretty big."

Nurse Caulfield was right. Sara had changed so quickly from a thin girl with a protruding pouch to a bulky pregnant woman.

"This is a symbolic act. So just lunge."

Gail lunged and speared Sara's fetus.

"Don't!" shrieked Cookie from the sidelines. "Not *there!*"

"She's right," said Gail. "I think if I knife her baby it might detract from the theme."

"Then why not stab her a little higher?"

"But if I get her in the shoulder I'll just wound her and she'd lie there screaming, not dying, and the death scene is the major symbol."

She made a good point. "Then try turning around," I suggested to Sara. "She can stab you in the back."

"But that wouldn't be a con*front*ation, would it?" said Gail. "That would change the whole symbolism. Why don't I forget the knife and hit her with a rock?"

It was stifling in the living room and they were getting hot and giggly. "Somebody open a door," I suggested. I didn't want anyone fainting before I had a complete run-through. And I didn't want to stop while they were enthusiastic.

"She could strangle me." Sara laughed hysterically. "That would be good and Shakespearian."

"I could spill poison in the 'porches of her ears.' " Gail giggled. "Or I could cut her wrists and her blood would drain into a large pot while she says her final lines!"

"She could lasso my ankles and clobber me as I fall!"

"And the multitudes can wash up to the elbows in the blood and cry out with their purpled hands the way they do in *Julius Caesar*."

They both collapsed exhausted with laughter on the sofa. That was all right. It was a beginning.

"If *some* people wouldn't be so *silly*," said Cookie, "there are other people who would like to rehearse."

Cookie was preparing herself for her role as the crippled girl in *The Glass Menagerie* by twisting her body around so that she was standing with one foot resting on the other and her bosom twisted upward, her shoulders turned to one side.

"What are you doing?" asked Helen.

"I'm showing my best side," said Cookie. "My left bust is bigger than my right."

"They both look pretty big to me," said Helen. "Why don't you just start."

"And remember," I said, "that this is a sad, frightened crippled girl who has embarrassed herself by throwing up in the classroom and instead of going back to school she spends the whole day walking in the park. We want to empathize with her problem."

"Then she shouldn't be walking in the park," said Cookie.

"She ought to be going to the movies or something to have a little fun and rest her crippled foot."

"But she's a *poor* crippled girl, Cookie. The central issue of the play is her poverty and what it does to her spirit."

"She could go to a second run. You'd be surprised how easy she could get into the show. She could stay outside all crippled and pitiful and some nice man would pay her way in."

"A *crippled* girl?" asked Mary Lou from the sidelines.

"Men *like* peculiar odd types," said Cookie knowledgeably. "A crippled girl can get a husband easier than a straight girl. I knew a girl once with a short arm . . ."

"Cookie," I directed, "read the lines."

"Okay," she said, taking her dramatic stance, "but I'm changing the ending."

"What do you *mean* you're changing the ending!"

"Why shouldn't I? You said we should empathize with the character. I feel sorry for her. She shouldn't let her mother make her feel lousy like that. She should fix herself up with a padded bra and some false eyelashes and she should get the boy."

"Cookie," I protested, "you can't change the ending of a play by Tennessee Williams. It's not done! You're missing the whole point of drama!"

"The point as *your* generation sees it!" Sara accused me. "Let her change it. Can't you see that she really cares? You preach empathy for a month and then you back down when somebody tries to do it."

"But you have to understand that this is the way Tennessee Williams sees women!"

"Well," said Cookie, "maybe they don't understand women in Tennessee."

"He understands women," said Gail. "He just doesn't like women. He's a fairy."

"Who's a fairy?" asked Helen.

"What's a fairy?" asked Baby, who had been slouching in a chair soaking up the entire conversation.

"Is *this* what she calls education?" whispered Doris hoarsely to Miss Rodriguiz from the open doorway.

That was the end of the first rehearsal. But I was not discouraged. For the first time my girls were totally involved. And the process was as important as the result.

So there was no necessity of discussing it with J. When my Huntington Players put on their polished performance for the whole house, with Doris and Miss Rodriguiz and the old secretary all in the audience, watching my players transformed from an awkward, self-absorbed group into a fine little troupe, *then* I would describe it to him. I would have the pleasure of seeing Miss Rodriguiz make a little note on her clipboard. And the pleasure of having Doris eat her words for once.

Not that I am vindictive. I simply believe in justice.

So I had no reason to be discouraged, had I?

By the second rehearsal they were all in the thrall of the stage.

"We worked out the killing," said a laughing Sara. And I was happy to see her livelier. The girls had been giggling over rehearsals for days. I could sense a new feeling of unity. But that was not enough. No. It was catharsis I wanted. Nothing less.

Sara and Gail took their places on center stage, next to the piano bench and the schefflera. Gail raised her arm and poised the rubber knife to strike.

"Wait!" screamed Baby and Marlene, who had come in carrying butcher paper between them on which a park had been childishly painted.

Doris marched behind them. "No thumbtacks," she cautioned.

They maneuvered around the cast, ran to the fireplace, hastily Scotch-Taped their scenery to the fireplace wall. But their little arms wouldn't reach high enough. The park was exceedingly low. Happily satisfied, they curled up together on the sofa to watch.

Gail raised her rubber knife. Sara raised her arm to fend off the blow. She moved a languid half-turn so that the weapon entered her side in a small unpregnant spot on her upper ribs. While she clutched the knife, Gail guided her down to her knees and she fell carefully while executing another half-turn and landed safely on her back to die, her eyes directed upward and her stomach a gently sloping landscape.

Gail stared down at her victim in mock alarm and moaned, according to script, "Oh my God, oh my God!"

Sara half raised herself off the floor, placed a hand on her stomach, a look of genuine amazement, a beautiful piece of acting, as if suddenly she had seen Truth.

"It moved!" she cried in astonishment. "My baby moved inside me."

"Big deal," said Cookie. "I need to rehearse my scene some more. I need to practice."

"Maybe it's trying to peck its way out of the shell," said Gail, helping Sara to her feet.

"I never believed it would feel so odd," said Sara in wonder.

Gail was shifting roles for Cookie's performance. Now she was the carping mother and Sara, rising from the floor somehow changed, shaking her hair in disbelief, eyes half-closed in introspection, moved toward the scene while she was still enveloped in a scene of her own. Yes. I could see it. They were becoming proper actresses.

"It's a very odd play," commented Doris. "Odd," echoed the old secretary, who had even brought in her own chair to watch the performance. Miss Rodriguiz joined them. A small but critical audience. I signaled the next scene to begin.

Gail opened with the words of the domineering mother, angering her son with her close attention to his eating habits.

"Chew . . . chew . . ." she carped. "Chew your food and give your salivary glands a chance to function!"

Sara revived herself. She became the brother, suddenly boyish and loose, almost the way she was when I met her, her free knapsack self. She looked at the mother with vicious intent.

"My enemies plan to dynamite this place. They're going to blow us all sky-high some night. And I'll be glad. You'll go up on a broomstick, you ugly babbling old witch!"

She'd missed some lines but she was perfect, absolutely perfect. Who was the mother to this girl? Who was the old witch that could make Sara read those lines as if she meant them?

"Didn't she edit the play?" asked Doris hoarsely. "What sort of play is this?"

Cookie came limping onstage, trying to remember which foot was crippled. She pulled her chest up, ready to deliver the lines which we had carefully rehearsed in the classroom all week, at which I thought she was becoming rather good. She opened her mouth, saw the eyes of the little audience focused on her, the small expectant audience. No words came. Cookie was frozen.

"The speech," I prompted her. "About how you threw up in class."

"What sort of plays are these?" rasped Doris. "Where did she find such trash?"

Cookie stood in abject terror, petrified by the audience of three. The backdrops, attached with Scotch Tape which had gone too dry, dropped.

"Cookie, don't let the small audience upset you. We'll have the whole house for the real performance. They'll love you. Just think of your lines."

"I'm not going to do it with people watching!" she was finally able to mutter. "You didn't tell me that there were going to be people watching!"

"If she's not going to do it I'm not," said Mary Lou.

"Cookie," I begged, "don't let the whole cast down. You can do it if you try."

She tried. She couldn't.

"I warned you," said Miss Rodriguiz, making a note on her damned clipboard.

"One more try," I begged them. "We're on the threshold! We're almost there!"

But most of my cast had already drifted off. A disappointed Baby and Marlene dragged off their painted park. Only Sara and Gail and I remained in the airless room. Gail had already opened a book and left us. Sara was collapsed on the heavy itchy sofa, her face pressed into the cut pile. I sat on the bench beside the schefflera wondering what to do next. Sara turned to me finally and I could see her face wet with tears, the blond hair stuck against her mouth.

"He's not coming, is he?" She looked up at me for denial.

I would have preferred the caustic comment. I didn't know what to do with tears. And I never knew whether her questions were rhetorical or not. And how did I know if the bus was coming? Probably not, after all those weeks.

"I'm not any better off than the crippled girl," she wept. "My heart's sick. There isn't any more air to breathe. He's not coming back."

It made me angry to see her lying there wounded, such a lively animal, lifeless and forlorn because a VW camping bus didn't drive into the driveway. Gail lowered her book for a moment, her own face contorted in distress, and then submerged again behind the pages.

Why were they so passive about accepting their defeat, sitting in their chairs day after day slumped over those bellies? I wanted them to come alive. I wanted them to be in control of themselves. I offered them catharsis and they didn't take it. Sara looked at me for a word. But I wasn't about to play God to an adolescent mother. It was too risky. I wasn't about to make decisions for a wildflower who suddenly found herself in a walled garden. No matter how much sympathy I felt for her. Or empathy. They had no logic, none of them.

"Try to see things in proportion, Sara," I told her. "This is just an episode. A single act. Like our play. It isn't the whole play after all. What's painful in this act may be joyful in the next." I thought my figure of speech very apt.

She looked up at me, horrified. "But I love him! Can you understand that I *love* him?"

.

"She loves him," I reported to J. "She's asked me over and over what I think love is. She should see that it can also be a biological trap. Don't you think?"

"Forget it," said J. "Forget love. We can't discuss love."

"Why can't we discuss love? It doesn't have to be personal. Two intelligent people can discuss anything, otherwise they can't have much of a relationship, can they?"

"Right," he said. "Good. Let's talk about philosophers and authors on the subject of love. Or major English poets on the subject of love. But love itself is non-discursive."

"Are you being sarcastic?"

"Not at all," he said airily. "Stick to your books. You could write a ten-thousand-word essay on the subject of love without batting an eyelash. So write it. Only don't advise pregnant girls on the logic of love!"

"That's my point!" He exasperated me. "If they understood the logic of it they wouldn't be in all this trouble!"

"You don't have to be sixteen and pregnant to be in trouble."

We both hung up.

The next day I started my unit on Logic and The Essay.

The Essay

SOME OF THE GIRLS looked up momentarily from their compositions as Doris opened the door and tiptoed heavy-footed to my
desk, trying not to disturb them.

"Can you do anything for this girl?" she whispered as she
handed me an enrollment card on which the name Marilyn was
barely discernible in the hills and valleys of letters laboriously
drawn.

"This girl" fluttered frightened in the doorway, a ragged
Kewpie doll with pimples. The nervous smile showed uneven
teeth crowding each other. Feathery yellow hair fell against her
face. Her hem was down.

Cookie came quickly to the heart of the matter. "Boy, she
should fix herself up."

"The poor thing is at the end of her pregnancy," explained
Doris hoarsely behind a cupped hand, "but the family has lit-
erally thrown her out until she delivers. She won't be with us
long enough to earn any credits but I thought you might be able
to do something for her."

"Hasn't your generation done enough for her already?" asked
Sara without removing her eyes from her essay.

I would have been delighted that Sara was actually doing my
assignment, except for the fact that she was crying as she wrote,

not noisily but wetly, the drops falling from her face onto the paper. She made no attempt to dry them and I made every attempt not to see them. Not because I empathized. I didn't even sympathize. Crying on an essay was simply ludicrous. What good did it do to cry on a theme paper?

But Marilyn was my momentary concern. She entered our essay unit apologetically, as if she realized that she wasn't official. She surveyed the room for a place that would be hospitable to her. Marlene and Baby were hard at work describing a horse and a dog they knew. Mary Lou bent stiffly over her paper to preserve the stability of her coiffure. Marilyn was evidently attracted to that elegant head and took an adjacent seat, glancing apprehensively at Mary Lou's almost filled page. Carefully she read the list of topics on the board, forming the words soundlessly with her lips, and picking at a pimple until it bled.

"I don't think I can do it," she explained. "I never wrote nothing before."

"Don't worry," Cookie consoled her. "You'll be okay as soon as you fix yourself up."

I left her with the problem of a topic and I circulated the room, starting as far from Sara as I could, reading paragraphs and making suggestions as I went.

SEA URCHINS
by
Mary Lou C.

Mrs. Miller does this sea urchin thing in class. The sea urchin is a kind of thing with things around it. It doesn't look like a fish but she says it is. You can't tell a female from a man except one makes eggs and the other makes sperms. A sperm looks like a worm but more active. Millions of sperms shoot at this one egg. I don't think humans have so many because there are more fish than people. One sperm gets on one egg. Then before you can say Jack Robin-hood it builds a wall. If another sperm pushes it can't get in because somebody is in there already. That makes another sea urchin. I don't think the Catholics would go for this because Life is the Work of the Creator. And the Sisters didn't teach this kind of science.

"Can't you find another word for *thing*?" I suggested. "Thing isn't very concrete and you overuse it."

She circled a number of *thing*s. "You better tell Sara to watch it," she mumbled into her paper. "She's in my room and I don't want any trouble."

"Watch what?" I whispered. But she was busy scratching *thing*s out. I glanced at Sara. The tears fell silently. But dramatically.

I turned to Gail's paper with anticipation. She had the makings of a first-rate literary critic. And so her topic surprised me.

RUMINATIONS ON A DEAD CAT

I don't know where the cat came from, how it came to that wire or how long it had been there when I came upon it. Very long I think. It had arrived unsuspecting, climbing as cats do. When it hit the wire it must have been electrocuted, openmouthed with amazement—wide cat eyes, splayed cat feet, hanging on to that wire. With time the sun dried it until it became a leather cat, balanced in eternal leathery surprise. It was always there as I past under it, startled and voiceless.

"Leathery surprise is wonderful," I told her. "But I don't understand your modification. Who was startled and voiceless, you or the cat? And you misspelled *passed*."

"That's one of the things I forgot," she said, pulling at her lip, a gesture I had not associated with Gail before. "Mea culpa.

I've forgotten the dumbest words. Like *surprise*. Was I right to put in an r?"

"Do you mean to tell me that you've read the complete Shakespeare, even *Cymbeline,* and you're fluent in Latin and you can't spell *passed?*"

"Only since the shock treatments. I forget odd things. Like French. I used to read Baudelaire and Hugo in the original." Her face flushed with anxiety as she spoke.

Sara must have been listening, because suddenly she was at Gail's side, embracing her. "Leave her alone. Her mother did it. She took Gail to a rotten shrink and they plugged her in and almost killed her."

"My mother meant well," objected Gail. "She thought it would help my depression. But all it did was make me forget my French."

"She's going to remember," said Sara. "We read French every night."

"That's not all she does every night," muttered Mary Lou. Sara threw her a caustic glance and turned back to me, but her eyes were ambiguous. Her voice was critical but the eyes were frightened.

"She's going to remember," she said to me, "in spite of your generation."

I was becoming accustomed to Sara's assault but the thought of the shock treatments upset me. "Don't lump us all together because we're older than you, Sara. I want her to remember her French too."

"Molto grazie," said Gail, relaxing a little. "It's a good thing I still remember my Italian."

"Why can't I write about something interesting like A Day at the Park, or something?" wailed Cookie. "I can't write about this junk!"

"Because," I explained to her, "I'm not the sort of teacher who gives silly topics like A Day in the Park or My Summer Vacation."

"Why not? I went to Lake Arrowhead for my summer vacation. I think my F.O.B. was there."

"What do you mean, you think?" asked Helen, looking up from her paper.

"I gave Welfare the whole list. I thought they could make them all contribute something. That's the *least* they could do."

"Better write about a day in the park," I told her.

A DAY IN THE PARK
by
Laverne A.
* * * * COOKIE * * * *

Parks these days are really not good. A person ought to have more privasy at a park. Shouldn't he? On my last pass my boyfriend took me to this park. The whole time you could hear cars on the freeway. The cars couldn't see us because we were behind a tree. *Try* to find a tree big enough these days! We set up these three trash cans for some privasy. And they had trash in them! The whole time you could hear cars on the freeway. Parks should be more private. What are we paying taxes for anyway?

I was happy to move to Helen's apparent book review. Which surprised me because she had not read any book that I remembered.

Ernest Hemingway's book, clearly written though nowhere exhilirating talks about happenings in the imagination where world's collide. He is right to dwell on Tortilla Flat and what he says thereabouts all points in the right direction. The pause at the end of a tied line which is not a complete syntactic unit creates an expectant silence.

I try to be flexible in my teaching but I can't tolerate plagiarism.

"What's this?" I asked her.

"A book report."

"You wrote this yourself?"

"It's my handwriting, isn't it?"

"I mean did you compose it yourself?"

"Yes."

"How do you know enough about Ernest Hemingway to call him exhilarating? What does exhilarating mean?"

"If you don't know what it means," she said defensively, "how come you're an English teacher?"

"Come on, Helen. You didn't write this."

"I *did* write it but you said we could do research and I did research and I used my own words."

"Tortilla and Flat are your own words. Ernest Hemingway didn't even write *Tortilla Flat*."

"Yes, he did. He wrote it and I wrote it and I want my credit."

It was a confrontation. And a confrontation between teacher and student is unforgivable. Everybody stopped to watch. And listen. Except for Marilyn, who had evidently found a compatible topic. She bent over her paper, knuckles tense as they gripped the pen, her nose almost touching the table.

The act of teaching demands constant adjustment.

"Helen," I said in a softer tone, "you're forever writing letters. Why not write an essay or a character study about the person to whom you write all those letters."

"If she doesn't stop that *whom* crap," wailed Sara, "I'm going out of my mind!" She slammed the desk as she got up, dragged herself across the room to her window, took a dried crust from her pocket and scraped it against the rusty screen. "I'm dying in this place!"

"She should look to her Heavenly Father for help instead of *you know what!*" said Mary Lou.

"Shut up!" shouted Sara shrilly. Immediately she berated herself, threw down the remaining crust, stood gripping her stomach. "I'm sorry, Mary Lou. I didn't mean it. I'm going back to bed."

Gail put down her pen and gave me a look of explanation, left in her wake.

The others checked the clock. The hour was almost up and they were finished. Only Marilyn sat with pen in hand, making her highs and lows. Her hair dragged on the paper.

"I didn't mean to make her mad," said Mary Lou, herself on the verge of tears. "I just don't want her to get in any trouble. If my boyfriend gets a three-day pass he's going to take me to visit his mother. And I don't want any trouble so I can't go."

They left. All but Marilyn who bent over her desk.

A grand lesson. Some juvenile paragraphs, one psychiatric daydream, one bogus book report, and two hysterical fits. If I ever got a first-rate essay I'd have a riot on my hands.

Marilyn proudly placed her finished product on my desk.

My Dog
by
Marilyn G.

Trixy is my sisters dog but I wish she was mine she is kewt and runs alot only she likes my sister beter then me. I wish she was mine.

"What grade do I get?" she asked anxiously, watching my eyes.

I floundered, trying to evade the question. But she was the only student who was showing any genuine interest. And I wanted to teach somebody something.

"Do you really want a grade on your first effort?" I asked her. "You've made a good start and what you need now is experience. The more you write the better you write."

"I want to show my sister," she pleaded, picking at a pimple.

I placed a courtesy C in red on the top of her essay.

"Keep writing," I said. "Take a topic a day and support it with clear, concrete examples."

She smiled at me, pleased with what I had said. "Nobody tried to teach me before. I'm going to try a lot." And she hesitated, a question on her lips, but she must have been fearful of the possible response.

"What?" I urged her.

"If I write every day, do you think I could get a B?"

"I don't see why not." After all, if she tried, why not?

"I never got a B," she said hopefully. "I'm going to work hard. My sister will be surprised."

I found Sara's essay where she had left it on her desk. The ink was smeared with tears.

.

"What do you mean you're teaching them the art of the paragraph!" said J. that evening. "Teach them psychology or religion or crocheting or birth control or something practical that will help them cope with disaster."

"That's what I've been trying to explain all week. Why don't you listen? To learn how to construct a logical paragraph is to learn how to cope with disaster."

"Don't get parallel with me," warned J.

"When you support a good generalization with clear concrete examples you learn how to think clearly and disaster can't overwhelm you. Just let me read Sara's paper. It's covered with tear spots. Believe me, after she finished she was able to see the implications, and the next time she writes on *this* topic she won't need to waste useless tears."

"And please don't read me paragraphs over the phone at eleven o'clock at night written by deserted pregnant teen-agers. And don't *ever* call tears useless. What do you know about tears to be qualified to say that tears are useless!"

"In a manner of speaking. Don't get so emotional. It disturbs your syntax. Just listen.

> There was a room where I was happy. Not just happy. Happiest. It was an old room but that didn't matter. The walls needed paint so we hung batik prints to cover the spots where the paint had peeled. I wanted to antique the chests but there wasn't any money. So I just scrubbed them and covered them with flowers. The table had a weak leg and he propped it with a book. We only had one chair so that we sat on the floor most of the time. He brought flowers from the fields. There was Indian Paintbrush and daisies. He put them in the milk pitcher because we didn't have any other place. The nut. Because I had to keep taking them out when we poured in the milk. He played his guitar and then he put it down to touch my face. He loved to put his hands on my face. I can feel the touch of his hand on my face this minute.

"Poor kid," said J. "Where's the boy now?"

"That's not the point. The point is that by developing a paragraph she can see the reality of that room without being misled by her emotions."

"But why? The most important room in her life and you want her to be logical!"

"You're as bad as she is. It was an unpainted, ill-furnished room and the boy who made her sit on the floor because he couldn't buy another chair ran out on her. Why romanticize it? Why cloud the truth with emotion?"

"Because life *is* emotion, that's why! That's all that life is! Life is not a goddamned composition."

He hung up.

There is no point in trying to enlighten him on the merits of paragraphing. J. is a very inflexible man.

Follow the Leader

I FOUND three papers in my box the next morning. So at least three girls had spent the evening doing my assignments. And the day was fair and warm. How foolish to become discouraged simply because they didn't progress fast enough. Blame the impatience of my own youth. It would have spoiled Sara's argument.

Marlene's horse paragraph. Her jolly pony. And Mary Lou had written an essay about the ocean. An improvement. A *definite* improvement. The texture improved and the lyrical quality improved. Amateurish, yes. But I had said it and it was true: The more they wrote, the better they wrote. The day became brighter.

Marilyn's paper was the last of the three. I was reading it when Doris caught my arm.

"How are you managing with Marilyn? Has she written her first paragraph?"

"Overwritten, I think." I was reading a bad copy of Mary Lou's paper. The spelling was awful, the punctuation absent, but in essence, in theme, the exact paper.

"A clear case of plagiarism. She copied Mary Lou."

"The poor thing," said Doris. "Are you certain?"

"I did my graduate work in composition, Doris. I know plagiarism when I see plagiarism."

"Oh how sad," said Doris. "But she isn't working for credit so don't make a thing of it."

"I wasn't intending to make a thing of it. I just won't grade it."

"Certainly, do as you see fit. But the poor child has been through so much. Can you just keep her busy until she delivers?"

"She is busy. Copying."

"Just don't make an issue of it, and, by the way, was Sara in class yesterday? Miss Rodriguiz would like to be informed if Sara misses any class."

"Why?" I was still disturbed by Mary Lou's oblique warning.

"Sara is a troubled girl."

"Everybody in this place is a troubled girl. What specifically is the matter?"

"Ask Miss Rodriguiz. And you'll be careful with Marilyn, won't you."

"Doris, I am not insensitive."

.

But I was disappointed. When I reached my room Marilyn was already waiting for me. A reconstructed Marilyn. Lank hair piled and twisted and tortured where there was no natural curl. And a red mouth. She had Mary Lou's head and Cookie's lipstick. I don't know whose eyelashes. And her dress was hemmed.

"Did you read it?" she asked, searching my face for approval.

"Yes I read it."

I tried to be as noncommittal as I could. But I placed the papers on my desk and unfortunately hers was on top. She looked for the grade.

"There isn't any mark on it."

"No," I answered simply. I wasn't going to make an issue.

"Why? Didn't I tell it right? I wrote about the ocean."

"It was a good subject, Marilyn. There are a number of misspelled words." Quickly I circled a couple of misspelled words.

She was relieved. "I don't spell so good. If I look them up, can I have my grade?"

I stalled, searching for a solution. "I thought it might be good experience for you to write in class today. It's good practice to try the same topic twice. To see how your ideas flower and expand. The more you write, the better you write."

My words were a terrible disappointment to her. "What did I do wrong? What else after the spelling?"

What else could I tell her without making an issue?

"I like this school," she said. "I never liked school before."

"Good. Very good. Then you can afford to take a chance and try to have confidence in your own ideas. I mean at first you might find yourself leaning just a little bit to the ideas of those with more experience. Until you get confidence. There's nothing wrong with that. And when you come to realize that you can do it yourself, you'll strike out on your own. I'm sure you will."

I said my piece as covertly as I could, but her face reflected that she knew exactly what I meant. She froze. The color drained, the pale blotched skin grayish against the bright Cookie lipstick.

"What did I do?" she asked faintly. "What did I do?"

I couldn't lie to her. "You might have taken some of Mary Lou's ideas. Not that you meant to. We often sort of think along with people when we're working close to them."

"I never!" she cried out passionately.

"Look Marilyn, the grade isn't important. It's what you learn that counts."

"People always say I do things I don't do. Why do they blame me? I never copied her! I worked the whole night on that paper!"

She was lying. Mary Lou was no Hemingway but she had a clear topic sentence and support statements. She didn't like the ocean. The empty beach was scary. The water sloshed. The wind made noises on the sand. Three support statements. Poor Mary Lou waiting for her invisible soldier. The shape and the texture of it were definitely Mary Lou.

"I never copied!" Marilyn cried out. "And I never took my sister's scarves and jewelry! She lied about them! And I never stole the pen! They lied! All of them! They always lie about me!" She ran from the room crying.

And I was filled with regret. She had cheated. But why was it *my* responsibility to make the scales balance? I could have put a B on her paper and that would have been that. So I'd compromise a little. Rather hurt my own conscience than cause her anguish over a stupid paragraph. But then I would have rewarded her for cheating.

I mean, what did they want me to do!

Mary Lou stuck her head into the room. Pearls and curls. "My boyfriend had to go to his cousin's yesterday. But he might come today. If he comes I'm leaving early."

And I was angry with Mary Lou. It was her fault as much as it was mine.

"It wasn't kind of you to let Marilyn copy your paper. She has to learn to do her own work. You weren't doing her any favor."

"Who copied what?" she asked.

"You let her copy your paragraph."

"No, I didn't."

"You mean you both accidentally wrote the same paper? Come on, Mary Lou."

"She didn't copy mine. I copied hers. I already said ten Hail Marys for it."

"What do you mean you copied hers!"

"I had a lot of science to do and I needed to wash my hair. I have a solid C-plus so you can go ahead and fail me. It averages in."

"How could you have copied hers? You had a clear topic sentence and three supports!"

"She knows more about the ocean than me. She has good ideas only she can't write so good. I took her paper and I cleaned it up and I added the support. Like you taught us."

"The spelling! And the punctuation!"

"Her grandmother is a fortuneteller on the pier. And her sister also. They always kick her out of the house and she has to sit on the empty beach sometimes all night by herself. It's creepy. You can fail me. I'll do another penance for it. And I'll tell in Confession. If my boyfriend comes I'm leaving early."

I could scarcely teach my first period class. As they worked silently I reread Marilyn's paper. I plowed through the impediments of calligraphy, the misplaced diphthongs, the poor alignment. The sea and the waves and the ghost steps and the empty sand. Her heart was right there and I had missed it. They should have stripped me of my credential. I should have been jeered out of the service. The horror of my awful misjudgment.

Where was I to take this terrible error for rectification? To Doris? She half expected men to stomp in from Downtown and haul me off for interrogation. To Miss Rodriguiz? And let her make notes on her clipboard to use for her next case study in a psychology seminar?

I had made an error of the heart and there was nowhere else to turn. I went down to an empty office and closed the door and called J. At nine-fifteen in the morning.

"What's wrong?" he asked, alarmed.

"I made a terrible mistake."

"What else?"

"I accused Marilyn of cheating and she's innocent. What am I going to do?"

"Oh," he moaned. "Poor kid."

"I know. It was a terrible thing to do to her. But I was absolutely certain she copied. All the evidence. And her spelling."

"Not her," he said. "She's used to it. She's probably been beaten up so often she expects it. It's you I'm sorry for."

.

I sat with Marilyn in the kitchen where Lucy had supplied us with milk and chocolate cake. I pushed the cake toward her.

"Honest to God, I'm sorry, Marilyn. I didn't realize the full extent of your originality. I was blinded by your lousy spelling."

"I'm trying real hard," she said. "I'm trying a lot."

"I know you are."

"I think I'm improving."

"I think so too."

She looked at me over the cake. Her baby mouth, the childish bow of her lips, the eyes still swollen from crying. She leaned toward me and touched my hand.

"I never took the scarves," she said with sincerity. "I never did."

.

I must have been rather subdued during second period. The girls worked silently. Marilyn scratched away in her awkward fashion. Mary Lou twisted one of her elaborate curls as she wrote. And Sara stared at her paper, an unused pen hanging from her fingers. There were circles under her eyes, as if she had not slept. All the tan she had brought with her from the forest streams was gone, a faded plant deprived of its life-giving sun.

But at the end of the hour she lingered over my desk.

"What's the matter with you anyhow?" she asked me. "Is our rotten writing depressing you or what?"

I couldn't be evasive with Sara. "I did something unfair to someone and I feel guilty."

"Good," she said, and she turned to go.

"Why is it good?" I called after her sharply. I was tired of being the target. I wasn't a stone after all. For them to take potshots at when they felt like it.

She turned, surprised that I was annoyed. She came back to my desk, patted me on the shoulder the way a master pets a sulky dog.

"No. I mean good that you feel. You've got to start somewhere, don't you."

The Valiant Sperm
and the Wonderful Vessel of God

Starch!" I exclaimed to Nurse Caulfield. "Why would anyone want to eat starch!"

"Don't ask me. Some of them like the taste of it. Or they think it's good for their babies. We haven't had a starch eater for two years. Dr. Lewin is hysterical. He wants all the girls upstairs for a starch lecture."

"He can't! This is my *Caesar* final. We've been preparing all week. They're in prime condition!"

"Don't complain," she said. "If he knew we had a pot smoker he'd have an apoplectic fit."

"Who's smoking?" I asked impulsively. As if I didn't immediately guess.

"You know who's smoking. And if she doesn't cut it out before somebody *official* finds out, she's going to be bounced. So if you don't want her to have that baby in a ward of the General Hospital you could just drop her a hint."

Not I. Nothing could induce me to get mixed up in that tangle of worms.

"You're the nurse. Give her a lecture on the misuse of drugs. That's your department, not mine."

She laughed at me. "Sara's not taking drugs. She's just smoking a little because she won't face facts. That baby is there to stay. She can't smoke it away. So just give your buddy a gentle nudge."

"And Sara isn't my personal friend. She's just my student." Which was not true. Student implied that I was teaching her something.

"Use a little tact," suggested Nurse Caulfield. "Just slip it to her that there are eyes watching. And if you really want to teach them something, teach them how to spot old wives' tales. Look, give the Indian maiden a little warning. Okay?"

Sara was not my problem. But the old wives' tales were. Dr. Lewin's lecture gave me a chance to ponder it.

Starch! Argo starch! Meant for stiffening materials prior to ironing! What are you doing to yourselves? What criminal way are you treating your bodies? Are you living in abject poverty where there is no food? There is food here. A flower needs soil with nutrients. You are the flowers! Do you ever listen to your bodies? Give me iron! Give me calcium! Give me B¹. But did you ever hear your bodies crying for Argo starch?

Who said that?

Please. Don't upset me. Treat yourself with respect. You are vessels of human creation. You are the highest form on the evolutionary ladder. Each swelling uterus is the miracle of life on earth. A sperm, a single sperm from the hordes of sperm, has switched his whiplike tail and begun his valiant voyage of exploration up that Fallopian tube to meet his wondrous egg. And who would dare defile this sacred vessel with starch!

"The point he was trying to make," I explained, "is that starch has no nutritional value."

"He was talking about love, not starch," said a bleary Sara.

"Actually," said Gail, "he was presenting a philosophical problem. Is man just an animal somewhere on the evolutionary ladder or is he the physical embodiment of the Spirit of God?"

"He's an animal," said Cookie. "Just ask me."

"Or like Caliban," said Gail, pulling at her lip, "half animal and half man. To show that part of us is rooted in the animal passions."

"I know which *half*," said Cookie.

"The spirit of God is only nature," stated Sara, fiddling with something suspicious inside her shirt pocket. Washed-out Sara. No more a lustrous stone. Just a dry colorless rock. "Your Holy Mary was only an unwed mother herself," she said. "The whole symbolism of the cross is a penis. You know that, don't you."

"That's blasphemy!" yelled Mary Lou. "She's going to get it. Just wait."

"If you want to know what's really true," I told them, "you'll have to learn a method of proving whether a statement is valid or not."

"When Zeus came to Leda," said Gail, "he came in the form of a bird and he impregnated Leda in a flutter of wings."

"With a *bird?*" asked Cookie. "She did it with a bird?"

"That's a myth," I said. "Just like the old wives' tale about the starch. And it's up to us as seekers of truth to test the logic in a scientific way."

"I believe in bird spirits," Sara broke in mischievously. She leaned toward the ledge that housed her doves. "Indians smoked peyote to talk with the bird spirits." She looked for my reaction.

No. I was not about to be drawn into a confrontation. Not on that subject. But before I could respond, she turned her back on me and began to sing.

> *If I could be a little sparrow*
> *If I had wings and I could fly*
> *I'd fly to the arms of my false lover*
> *And when he'd speak I would surely die.*

"It isn't beautiful like vessels," said Cookie bitterly. "When you're pregnant they shoot you full of stuff and pop you with pills and ram their hairy arms up you. And you can't have any more fun. You can't even lift your arms over your head or you'll tie the cord around your baby's neck."

"Cookie, that's exactly what I'm talking about. That's an old wives' tale. It's not true."

"It is so true," she protested. "Everybody knows it's true. And my aunt told me. And she's not old and she's not a wife."

"Just because everybody knows it doesn't make it so."

"Who says?" asked Cookie. "If you let a dog lick you when you're pregnant you give your baby black birthmarks."

"Can't I even let my dog kiss me?" cried Baby, alarmed. "If I get my dog can't I even let it kiss me?"

"What about horses?" asked Marlene. "Can you get spots from horses?"

"The devil can mark your baby," said Marilyn softly from her seat, frowning and scratching her acne. "My sister told me that."

"I know a girl," said Helen confidentially, "who ate ice cream every day she was pregnant and when her baby was born it had an ice-cream-cone-shaped spot on its forehead."

"That's exactly what I mean," I insisted. "By the time you've eaten an ice cream cone it's all mush, isn't it? It hasn't any shape left. Where's the logic of it?"

"She always thinks she's so right," said Cookie, addressing the group. "She told us to prove things from our experience, didn't she?"

"Good for you, Cookie. Exactly. That's the first step in logical thinking."

"Well," she announced, smiling and looking about for confirmation. "Did she ever have a baby?"

My silence was reply enough.

"Am I having a baby?" she asked smugly.

"Yes, I agree that Cookie is having a baby, but what does that prove?"

"Dr. Lewin said our babies cry for calcium. Did *you* ever hear a baby cry out in anybody?"

"Dr. Lewin was simply using a metaphor. He meant *cry out* in a manner of speaking."

"You mean he *lied*," said Cookie. "So," she said proudly, concluding her summary, "what I said was true." She rested her case.

Sara clapped her hands in delight, taking up Cookie's argument. "How about marijuana? Is marijuana good for you when you're pregnant?"

How could I avoid her? The class leaned forward for my response. "Certainly it's not good for you. Sara, if you read any clinical evidence . . ."

"I mean have you ever smoked any? Have you ever felt any? Have you ever let loose? Have you ever flown out of this rotten box?"

"Lethe and nepenthe," said Gail. "The mortal coil we shuffle off in dreams."

"Right," said Sara. "Have you ever smoked?"

"Look, there are certain things one doesn't actually have to try in order to understand the dangers . . . there are statistical studies . . ."

"*One* always reads statistical studies, doesn't *one!* Well, Cookie's aunt did a statistical study. So she's as right as you are!"

By the time she had played her game out she was angry. "I've got to get out of here. I'm drowning in this place. I've got to get to the ocean to breathe. Does anyone understand that?" She pushed away from the table and started for the door.

I was annoyed by her actions but Gail was alarmed. "Don't! Please!"

There was enough of an appeal in Gail's voice to force Sara reluctantly back to her chair. But she looked at me as if I were the cause, the force pinning her to earth. I wasn't going to keep her there. Not I. If she wanted to leave, let her take her own responsibility. And I had no intention of letting her make me feel guilty.

"I heard from somebody," said Helen, "that if you eat gingersnaps you can lose your baby."

And I had the rest of my class to consider.

"That's exactly the sort of statement we can check," I said. "If Helen had a control group and if one group ate gingersnaps and the other group didn't, then you might come up with a true statement."

"I already proved it," said Helen. "All I got was gas."

"The truth," said Gail solemnly, "is that love is the camouflage. Love changes animals to gods and that mixes it all up. I knew an animal once, just like all the other animals. That's what my mother calls them. Animals."

She silenced the class with her statement. Sara turned toward her in curious sympathy. I could see that Gail was trying to draw Sara back but I don't think she meant to say so much. The words tumbled out.

"Love was a sorcerer. It changed the world into something beautiful."

"When?" asked Sara softly. "You never said."

I tried to think of some way to keep the conversation on a less personal level. But Gail was playing her scene for Sara's benefit. And I could not stop her.

"When we read together," said Gail, drifting with Sara's interest, "the colors of the earth became more vibrant and the sky turned to fire. We read sonnets and triolets. The trees broke into bloom, and the grass."

"Grass does that," nodded Helen.

"You're all going to get into trouble," said Mary Lou. "I warned you."

I made a mental note to consult with Nurse Caulfield.

"I thought I was flying," said Gail, half in a dream, "right on the wings of the swan."

"Did you fly?" asked Sara eagerly. "Did the bird spirit possess you?"

Gail awoke. "I landed here," she said dryly. "All the sperm were disguised, like Shakespeare's villains, and nothing was what it seemed."

"You're not kidding," said Cookie. "The things they hide it with. That's why they do it in the dark. Old lousy sperm. They say beautiful things to make you fall in love and all the time those lousy sperm are just trying to make it."

"You're only supposed to do it to get a family," said Mary Lou. "It's a sin to do it for fun. It isn't that much fun anyway," she added, "and now I have this sin on my record."

"You wait in the hot sun for a blessing of rain from the gods," said Gail, "their absolution and their cooling waters." Suddenly she laughed. "And all they shower you with is a deluge of sperm."

"Watch it about Jesus," said Mary Lou. "He's only trying to teach us a lesson."

"What lesson!" demanded Sara. "Does Jesus want us to learn a unit in logic?"

I didn't answer but I suppose she could see my displeasure. She had ruined my lesson. And not the first time. What surprised me was that my displeasure seemed to wound her. What were the rules of this game?

"Where is he?" asked Sara gently, turning back to Gail.

"In the sanatorium. We thought we could lead each other through the maze, but it was a lie. My mother said it was a lie."

And then she asked me a question. "Was it the truth or was it an old wife's tale?"

Curious. I did not remember Gail's ever having asked me a question before. I wanted to answer her, in a way that would not be too subjective but that would give her some reassurance. Sara cut me off.

"Don't ask *her!* Don't trust *her* generation. Trust your intuition. Trust your heart!"

"Now *that,*" I said "is directly out of *my* generation. It's a statement from Emerson. Sara, how can we discuss logic when you cloud everything with emotion?"

She brushed me off with a shrug. "Where is he now?" she asked Gail.

"He's sick," Gail replied faintly.

"Then he needs you," stated Sara. "Can you phone him?"

"I wanted to," said Gail, rubbing her eyes, "but she won't let me."

"Your mother can't stop you from writing at least. She'll never know if you write him a letter."

"We won't tell," said Baby. "We didn't tell about the grass and we won't tell about that."

Suddenly she realized that she had spoken in my presence. Baby looked apprehensively from me to the group. "Will she tell?"

"Don't worry," said Helen confidently. "She won't."

The whole bunch of them! My clutch of seniors! They were all smoking! And they weren't worried about me. I had finally won their confidence. I couldn't get them to finish one lousy assignment but they knew I would not be a fink.

"Why can't you write to him?" pressed Sara.

"Because I forgot my French," said Gail.

"Why do you have to write in French?"

Gail's voice dropped to a whisper. "There's a reason. I can't remember why."

"If anyone touches your stomach except your F.O.B.," announced Cookie, "your baby will be born mental, and that's the truth."

"The truth," said Gail, "is that Leda's swan was half bird and half man. He was man's baser spirit and man's higher spirit. But all the birds have flown. All gone. Back into the book of myths. And we're nothing but empty vessels for a mess of valiant sperm."

There was a moment of silence while I tried to figure out a way to pull together the chaotic emotions that surrounded me. That pressed in on me. Sara broke the silence with her thin spontaneous melody.

> *I'd fly to the arms of my false lover*
> *I'd fly so high that I could see*
> *His cheating heart in a box of silver*
> *And I'd lock it up with a silver key.*

"I've got to get to the ocean now," she said urgently. "I've got to get into the surf and let the waves pound me. I'll die if I don't. I've got to climb out on a rock I know and see the breakers all by myself with the sun dying in the sky." She looked apologetically toward Gail. "Please," she said, "I've got to go now." She rose, looked to me, waiting to see if I would stop her.

"I'm going to leave by the kitchen door so no one will see me," she said. "Are you going to tell them I've gone?" She took a small hand-rolled cigarette from her pocket and stuck it behind her ear. "Come on," she taunted me. "Try and stop me with your logic."

Sara stood laughing at me, but through her bravado I saw her real face. She was in panic. "You won't tell," she answered for me. "Your generation is so disgustingly compassionate. It's your sense of guilt."

Guilty of what? She chose to play house on the redwood carpet of the forest floor, not I. I didn't swim naked in icy pools, because I knew the logical consequences. And I had a logical answer for her.

"If you go to the ocean now you risk getting thrown out of Huntington House. You're entitled to a weekend pass. Wait until Saturday and take a bus to the beach and you can watch the breakers then."

She looked at me, into me, searching for something. "How can I make you understand anything when you're crazy!"

She turned and ran for the stairs. And I sat and watched her go.

"Boy!" said Helen, returning to her letter.

"If she hurts her baby it will be a mortal sin," said Mary Lou.

Gail berated me with her eyes and then retreated behind a book.

This was bravado. It had to be. Earthbound Sara. She asked for logic. She got logic. But logic was not what she wanted. She wanted a boy in a VW bus. And that I could not give her. The pounding surf would not bring her that and my logic told her so. She would not stand in the surf. Not with that belly. She would lie on her bed and dream about forests. She would smoke with the door locked. And then she would be sorry. She called me crazy. Poor crazy Sara.

I turned my attention to the class. Cookie slumped dejectedly in her chair. "It tastes good when you're pregnant," she said.

"What?" I asked her. "Pot?"

"No. Starch."

"Cookie, are you the starch eater?"

"Why do *we* have to be the vessels?" she moaned, punching her enormous belly with one stumpy finger. "Why can't *they* be the vessels for once? It's just not fair."

Special Delivery

I'M DEPRESSED," I said to J.

"Are you," he answered. I changed the phone to my other hand as I tested to see whether my tea was ready to drink.

"I'm having tea and cinnamon toast," I told him.

"That's bad," he said. "Tea is bad. But cinnamon toast is really serious."

"I mean, what am I? They hired me as a teacher, not a psychiatrist. They hired me because I understood twentieth-century modern lit, not because I have a warm and sympathetic ear."

"I should hope not."

"What do you mean 'I should hope not' in that tone?"

"I mean that you haven't got a particularly warm manner and you haven't got a particularly sympathetic ear."

"Then why are you wasting your precious time on this phone?"

"You have saving graces."

"They simply don't realize the implications of anything they read or learn on their own lives. They ignore logic and rush headlong into disaster. They don't make connections."

"Maybe this isn't the time for them to make connections. Maybe this is the time for them to make babies."

"It's pressing in," I said.

"That means, I gather, that you're going to change jobs again."

"I have no intention of changing jobs. It's just that I'm trying to locate firm ground in this morass of illogical feelings."

"That's an interesting metaphor," he said, rather superciliously, I thought. "Why are feelings a morass? Why aren't feelings a warm and gentle sea? Don't fall in them, for God's sake, just float *on* them."

"One doesn't just float on water," I said, a bit annoyed, I admit. He knows I can't swim. "One can drown in water."

"Well then," he said in that tone he always assumes when he thinks he has the advantage, "take swimming lessons. Let a kind friend hold you up."

"Why is it," I asked him, "when I talk about teaching you always digress? You're worse than the girls."

"Okay," he said curtly, "I digress. You're not ready to float. Do you know why?"

"I'm too depressed to play parlor games."

"Because you've got a lump of stone somewhere. Why don't you dump it."

He hung up.

Really. Let a friend hold you up. When you can't even count on a friend to raise your spirits when you're in a tea-and-cinnamon-toast condition.

.

Sara's sad little song lingered with me the next morning. As my car crept along the clogged freeway I could still hear the small melody. It blended with the gray and damp. All promise of summer had disappeared. I had visions of Sara, drowned and bloated, washed up in the dank tide. And that was exactly the vision she wanted me to have. My guilty generation. No. She got pregnant by herself and she'd have to solve the problem by herself. What I needed was a new approach, something softer than the essay. There had to be a way to bring a raft of logic to girls drowning in feelings. And if that was a rotten metaphor, well it was a rotten morning.

The girls were still at breakfast when I arrived.

"Miserable day," complained the old secretary. She hadn't even cubed her ivy. "If you see Sara, tell her Miss Rodriguiz wants her."

Let Miss Rodriguiz read her own riot act. I turned to my box to see the day's notices. The mailman must have come early because the secretary was sorting the mail, stopping to flex the joints of her fingers which were also full of damp. Through the door I could see girls shuffling to or from breakfast, heavy-lidded, half-asleep. Some had evidently noticed the mail because stragglers from the dining room gathered about the desk, reaching for letters, scanning return addresses, drifting off to read. Or standing disappointed at the absence of correspondence. Helen was one of these.

Yet as I turned to walk upstairs I saw her lingering at the end of the corridor, holding a letter. I wondered what letter it was. She waved at me. "Hey!" she called. "Can you do something for me?"

And another "Hey!" but this time from the top of the stairs, and in distress. "Hey don't!" begged Marilyn. Still in her tattered nightgown and ratty robe, she was being edged forward by Nurse Caulfield who pushed hard behind her, squeezing her down the steps.

"Hey, not yet!" she protested, hanging on to the rail. "I don't want to go yet!"

"Honey, you've got to go. Your water is leaking all over the floor. Doctor Lewin is waiting at the hospital for you. I told you an hour ago to get dressed. So you'll have to go like this."

Girls circled the stairway to watch the show. "Lucky!" yelled somebody.

Cookie plodded to the foot of the steps. "Don't let them give you a Caesarean! Even if you're in labor twenty-four hours!"

"I don't want to go yet! My cards are bad! Let me cut the cards one more time!"

"Somebody go up and get her suitcase," said Nurse Caulfield.

"We will!" offered Baby and Marlene, edging around the two of them to climb the stairs.

"Just don't let them give you a spinal," counseled Cookie. "Take ether. A spinal gives you fits."

"Cookie," called Nurse Caulfield, "why don't you shut up."

Marilyn looked to the spectators for aid. Found none. Her eyes caught mine. "I liked it here," she said. And then to everybody, "I liked it here."

"She's crazy," said somebody.

Marilyn settled down on the steps with Nurse Caulfield beside her, arguing. Miss Rodriguiz came out of her office, making scratches on her clipboard.

"It's going to be one of those mornings," she said to me. "Have you seen Sara? I want to talk to her."

"I haven't seen Sara." I was annoyed. This was oppressive.

Baby and Marlene came down lugging Marilyn's shabby case. "Here's your things, Marilyn. Call us and tell if it hurts."

Marilyn reluctantly allowed herself to be led to the door. She turned and looked at the girls who were already moving off, concerned with their own affairs.

"Good luck, Marilyn," I called. "And keep writing!"

"Don't make it such a firm goodbye," said Miss Rodriguiz. "I have a feeling that she'll be back."

"You think it's only false labor? Her water bag is broken."

"Just her water bag? Did you see the look in her eyes? Why do you think girls have babies anyhow? This place is a mausoleum today. Is there a hot cup of coffee anywhere?" She headed for the kitchen. "If you wouldn't keep yourself so aloof," she called over her shoulder, "you'd know what was going on."

Aloof? Nobody could say that I was aloof. I was no ivory-tower teacher. I just wasn't gregarious. I was selective. What did she mean *aloof!*

Marilyn's cards were right. It was a bad day to start *The Bridge of San Luis Rey*. And I had quite forgotten Helen and her request until I saw her in second period, bent over a letter.

"Did anyone call Marilyn?" asked Baby. "Did she have it yet?"

"They don't come so soon," answered Cookie. "It takes hours of suffering. Sometimes days."

I was too dispirited to refute her.

"Today I want to start a novel called *The Bridge of San Luis Rey*. And I've chosen this novel because it asks an important question. Do you know what that question is?"

Certainly they didn't know what the question was. But I was wandering because my eyes had focused on Sara's empty chair. Was it possible that she had really gone to the ocean? And I had chosen not to plead with her to return! I searched the class for other expressions of alarm. Found none.

"The question is this," I continued, my eyes pinned to the empty chair, "is the universe and everything in it planned or un-planned?"

"Planned," said Cookie.

She surprised me. "When did you read the novel?"

"I didn't. You wanted us to choose one so I chose."

The empty chair. And nobody hysterical. Helen wrote calmly as she did through all my lectures. Gail behind her book. Baby and Marlene giving me rapt attention as they did for every lesson that wasn't aimed at them.

"Does anybody know," I asked with trepidation, "where is Sara?"

"Sick!" called two voices.

"She's ill," said Gail. She closed her book and laid it on the table, sat quietly with her hands clasped.

"Sick with what?"

"Just sick," said Helen, looking up. "Don't worry about it."

We opened the books and started the first chapter but I worried about it. And I wasn't the only one. Miss Rodriguiz looked in, scanned the room. "Where's Sara? Didn't she come to class today?"

"Sure she came to class," said Helen, "but she had to go to the bathroom. She had the runs so she's sitting on the can. You're not going to bother a person on the can, are you?"

"Certainly not. As long as she was in the class." She looked to me for confirmation. "One of the housemothers said she wasn't at breakfast and she isn't in her room and she missed first period."

"She has diarrhea," insisted Cookie, looking at me as she spoke, giving me a silent command. "Can't a person have diarrhea if she wants to?"

Miss Rodriguiz waited for me to comment. The girls rested their eyes on me, warning me most unmistakably to keep my mouth shut.

Sara! Even in her absence she managed to press in on me. And where was she? If I told the truth I might lose whatever feeble gains I had made with my seniors. And if I didn't, who knows what she might be doing to harm herself.

Miss Rodriguiz tapped her pencil against her clipboard. "Our rules are for the best interest of the girls. Remember that."

Sara stepped quietly into the room, pale as death, chilled and shoeless, her thin short shift damp and plastered to her bulging stomach.

"Did you call roll?" she asked, shivering as she spoke. "I was . . ."

"In the bathroom," yelled Helen. "We told her already."

"I was in the bathroom," she said through blue lips.

"What were you doing there?" asked Miss Rodriguiz. "Taking a shower in ice water? Go put some clothes on!" She surveyed Sara, the class, me. Gave me that I-hope-you-know-what-you're-doing look. "God, what a lousy day," she commented as she left.

Sara was surrounded. Gail took her hand, wiped her damp hair from her cheek. "I knew you'd come back. I knew you wouldn't leave me alone."

"I went to the sea," said Sara, beginning to weep. "I met some boys and they took me on a wild sea ride."

"Did you hurt your baby?" gasped Cookie.

"I think I killed it," she said, clasping her wet tight stomach. "It hurts me and my baby isn't moving anymore." She howled in agony. "I killed my baby!"

"Somebody go for Doctor Lewin," I called, leading her to a chair.

She sank into it, her arms listless at her sides, her head almost limp on her shoulders. "I can't feel my baby move," she moaned pitifully. "My baby doesn't move."

"It'll move," wept Baby, throwing her arms around Sara's neck. "It's just sleeping."

"Dr. Lewin is with Marilyn," Mary Lou reminded us. "Should we get a priest?"

"My baby will die," wept Sara. "Without even a name. She's a girl. Did you know she's a girl?" she begged me tearfully.

"Call the office," I told Helen. "Get someone up here."

"We'll make her live," said Gail, caressing Sara's stomach. "She was just lulled by the sirens the way you were."

"My daughter doesn't even have a name," she wept. She pulled her wet dress up to expose the naked swell of her belly. She patted it, crying on it. "Are you still there? Are you all right?" She moaned in pain. "I'm calling her Heather," she said between gasps of tears. "Because the open fields are so free. Happy birthday, Heather," she called, pressing her mouth toward her cold stomach.

"What the hell is going on here?" called Nurse Caulfield. "If it isn't one damn thing today it's another."

"I killed my baby," grieved Sara. "I named her Heather. She would have come camping with me in a back sling. She would have been with me forever!"

"Pull your clothes down and let's get you and Heather to bed. Babies don't kill so easy but somebody in this place is going to get murdered!"

She dragged Sara off, straightening her dress as they walked. Sara turned back to us. "Write my mother!" she called in her anguish. "Tell her I killed my baby!"

"You said your mother was dead," answered a startled Gail.

"She is!" called Sara from the hall. "They're both dead. They live in Omaha, Nebraska!"

I read *The Bridge of San Luis Rey* aloud for the hour. They listened in silence. Conspirators all. And all of us ached for a dead baby named Heather.

Helen lingered after they had left. "Hey, can you do something for me."

"If I can," I answered. Drained. My mind on Sara. Seeing Sara's face before she left. Hearing Sara's plea.

"See," she began, bringing a letter up to my desk, "the reason I'm not getting an answer is that I don't write so good. So if you make the corrections and show me how to say it better, he'll write me."

"Is this your F.O.B.?" I asked her. "I'll make the corrections for you, but I can't guarantee that he'll answer."

"Then what good is it to learn anything? It's to my father.

My last father. Who's married to my mother. Ada is my mother and she chased him off."

She shoved the letter, pencil-written and full of corrections and erasures, for my inspection, and she waited, watching my face as I read.

Dear Mike

I wrote and wrote but you didn't anser me. Ada says you run out but I don't beleive her. I know your in Santa Monica because Roxie saw you on the peer. So she knows you are with Phil. So I am sending this letter to Phil and he can give it to you. Im not mad at you. I know she chased you out. She always use to yell at me and my dad. Boy when she gets' mad. But you were always my freind. I never had such a good freind. The good times we use to have when we sat up and watched T.V. The good old gunsmoke and the good old startrek and them. Ha. Ha. Nobody comes to see me since you run out. Ada is mad and she won't come until *you know what* is give away. All she does is yell so I don't care. If you could just send me a poscard or something. To tell me if your mad. Im doing real good at school. You were the ony freind I had. I wont tell Ada you wrote if you write. You don't have to visit me. Just send a poscard.

> Your freind
> Helen

I didn't know where to start or what to add. I underlined *freind* and *poscard*.

"Make the grammar good," she said. "If I send him my report card at the end of the term he has to sign it and send it back to me, doesn't he? I mean it's the law you have to sign a report card, isn't it?"

I put a capital G on Gunsmoke. She turned over the letter for me. She had added a postscript.

P.S. After *you know what* is give away I could come and cook for you. Remember the cool hot dogs and the chili? That I made when we watched the late late? Ha. Ha. I'm even gratuating if I can get the credit. I would ask you to come but if you would just write it would be Ok. I sure would like to hear from you.

Goodby again.
Helen

"Should I send it special delivery?" she asked.

The Librarian

I DRANK TOO MUCH TEA and so I could not sleep. Sleepless, I had visions of eggs breaking and yielding up unborn fetuses, bloody and pitiful. When I slept finally, I had my old dream about the telephone. A long lonely corridor and the telephone and the darkness and the one coin and the madness of trying to put the coin in the slot, of losing it, of finding it, of the tremendous relief at the coin's falling into the box, the ringing, and then the sickening click as I disconnected.

I awoke fatigued. I drove the freeway in a blur of distress, remembering Sara, the appeal in her eyes as she asked me to stop her. And she wanted me to stop her. I was sure of that now. I climbed the steps to Huntington House, pausing at the turn, thinking back to that first day and the panicked girl and the vanishing VW bus. Of the door that closed behind us. Of the rock she had offered me. In a way I had refused that also.

Miss Rodriguiz and Nurse Caulfield were huddled in the little visitors' corner. I threw myself toward them. "Did they save the baby? What hospital is she in?"

"Who?" asked Miss Rodriguiz.

"Who! What do you mean *who!*"

"She means Sara," laughed Nurse Caulfield. "Don't let that Sara suck you in with her dramatics."

"What do you *mean* dramatics! She was having agonizing pains and her baby wasn't moving!"

"Babies in utero are not in constant motion and she had pains because she'd been sitting around in a hamburger joint with a bunch of beach bums and she got indigestion."

Miss Rodriguiz smiled indulgently. "Don't be so aloof. You'll learn the ropes."

So that by the time I reached the office I was steaming.

"Did you get my note about the visiting librarian?" asked Doris. "I can't see that we need a librarian with all those books upstairs. And the girls never seem to read them," she added. With overtones.

"*Yes*, we need a visiting librarian. Those books have been upstairs since the first stone was laid for this building. Everything is by Edgar Guest. If there were any *decent* books they'd be read!"

Oh yes. Trust J. Float on feelings. And on my first swim I get bogged down in this swamp!

And I was furious with Sara.

"But consider that the government will be paying for the librarian," said Doris, "and with the state of the world we can't expect the government to pay for every luxury. Personally I find the upstairs books very uplifting. Most of our modern novels are terribly negative. Have you noticed?"

"If the government goes out of its way to offer us a librarian, it must consider a librarian exceedingly important. The government doesn't make casual decisions, Doris."

"That's true," she said.

Yes. I wanted a librarian. Books were needed. Work and work sheets and questions to be answered. Tests were needed and quizzes. Enough dying ingénues. It was time for them to go to work.

"Do we want a visiting librarian?" I asked them in second period, angrily watching Sara out of the corner of my eye. She sat cheerily by her window in a fresh yellow shift, her hair all brushed out and tied with a ribbon, and *crocheting* something, *smiling* as she worked.

Gail gave the only whoop of enthusiasm. "From a respectable library? Can he get Hesse and Marcuse and Lamartine in translation? Can he get me a book on tarot cards?"

"I didn't know you could read the cards!" said Sara, alert and excited. "I have to make plans for Heather. Heather and I are going hiking as soon as she's old enough to sit in a sling and I want to know when he's coming back for us." She looked defiantly at me. "*When* he's coming back!" as if I had verbalized her doubts.

"I don't read the cards," said Gail. "I'm just interested in the symbolism."

"I'll take her to the woods when she's old enough and I'll teach her belly botany. We'll scrunch down together and we'll study the infinitesimally small plants. Her little fingers will feel the fuzzy leaves."

There was a general sigh for small baby fingers. "I'll nurse her by the quiet waters." Smiling at me in such a way as if she would nurse her baby under the mottled leaves in spite of me. She settled back in her chair like a fat pigeon, its ocean flight done, content and ready to nest.

"Heather will sleep in a cradle by our bed," said Sara, "and when we open our eyes in the morning the first thing we'll see will be her face smiling at us."

The subject for that hour was Heather. A monologue.

As they filed out at the end of the hour Sara paused at my desk. I had no desire to talk to her. About anything.

"Thanks for not telling," she said simply. "You know."

I looked up at her, searched her face for any hint of irony. She was absolutely sincere. I could swear it. She smiled indulgently at my puzzlement. "Don't worry," she advised me. "You worry too much. You know that, don't you."

·

"The girls are unanimous," I told Doris. "They're very enthusiastic. Get us a librarian."

·

He appeared at our door the following Monday with his book bag. Small, rather delicate, not much older than the girls, a charming smile, and as he entered the room it was obvious that he was lame. One stiff leg dragged after the good one. He crossed the room with effort, carrying his book bag over his shoulder like a sailor.

"I'm the bookman," he announced. "Wait until you see what I've brought. You want love? I've got love. You want mysteries? I've got mysteries. You want sex?" He winked roguishly. "I've got detective stories."

"I like him," announced Cookie. She spoke for the group. They followed the movement of his damaged leg with sympathy. With empathy.

He perched on the edge of my desk. "Ladies," he stated, "the world is in books. Freedom is in books."

"Don't tell my mother," said Gail.

"Or mine," said Sara, crocheting furiously. Who would be the mother of that grounded wood nymph? I could not imagine.

"My dear girls," he told them, "next to your confessor your librarian is the most discreet. Read what you will, to your heart's desire, your librarian will never tell."

"Don't bring those kind," said Mary Lou. "I'm in enough trouble with the Catholics already."

"Books are my job. I'm a dream-bringer. Do you see this book?" He held up one from the stack that he had dumped on my desk. "Two young boys wake in the middle of the night and hear weird music. Circus music, only it's playing backward. And a man gets on a merry-go-round and it's running backward. And when that man gets off, imagine what?"

"What?" asked Cookie eagerly. They were all leaning toward him. Actually in interest. He held out the book. "Read it. You'll see."

They all smiled warmly at him as they left. Sara stopped, poked her stomach out at him. "Her name is Heather. She's going camping with me in the woods and she'll be friends with the little animals."

He tapped her gently on the stomach. "Hello, little Heather. I'll bring you little books when you come."

Sara leaned toward me in confidence, spoke loud enough for him to hear. "Keep an eye on the librarian. You'll learn something."

All right. So to motivate them one needed to be an Adonis or a poor handicapped librarian. I was not jealous. I would watch him. And if he had tricks in his book bag I was willing to learn.

He sat with me to visit before my next class.

"They're dreamers, aren't they," he said. "I hope their dreams aren't too sad. Do they give up their babies?" he asked with much sympathy.

"Most do, as far as I know."

"Not the blond one," he said. "She needs it, doesn't she. Will she have anyone to take care of her and Heather?"

"I really don't know." I didn't. It had never occurred to me to ask.

He actually raised his eyebrows at me, as if I should. As if I should have at my fingertips information about her personal life. He expected me to drip with compassion for that actress. Well, I didn't feel compassionate. Not with her talent for histrionics. But his implication depressed me. I needed tea.

"Please," he said, touching my hand, "don't think that I'm being critical."

"I didn't say that you were being critical."

"I sensed it. Don't think that all my stops are as easy as this one. Stories appeal to dreamers. It's the hungry ones that pull at me. You can't believe the thrill I get at the library with some of these poor kids. For the first time, seeing them sparked by an exciting idea. And then to have them yanked out by the mommas and grandmothers. It pains me."

"Yanked out for what reason?"

"Because I'm a foreigner in this neighborhood and because I stir the kids up. Books do that. Makes them discontent. Pregnant girls can dream, but these hungry kids eat up everything and the abuelas give me trouble. They sit in judgment in their little black shawls and call my books instruments of evil. And my leg a punishment from the devil. I have one boy," he said, "who's a shark for learning. My wife and I took him to the museum. You should have seen him. Not gracious or appreciative you understand, like your girls, I suppose, but he went crazy with excitement. When the abuela found out she threatened to pull him out of my Great Books. Now when he comes she sits nearby watching me."

"But even when they give you a pain you don't give up."

"Not on your life." He smiled, drawing himself up to the full height of his short stature and his lame leg. "I, mademoiselle, am a librarian, and a librarian is not easily deterred. It's a part of the oath we swear. On a good book."

.

"He's wonderful," I told J. that evening. "I can't tell you how much I admire the way he captured their interest."

"Is that a fact," he said rather dryly.

"And the girls are receptive. They never notice his leg."

"What leg?"

"His crippled leg. They never look at it or mention it in any way. They're terribly tactful."

"But *you* notice it."

"The leg? Of course I don't. I never let on . . ."

"But you mentioned it to me, so you must have noticed it and you're tactfully avoiding it."

"You're in a rotten mood. What's the matter with you?"

"I'm not in the mood to discuss marvelous men you've met."

"The librarian? Don't be absurd. He's married."

"With all those wonderful plots and all those wonderful books and your eternal romance with the English department, it probably makes him all the more romantic. A gimpy sensitive bookbringer right out of Somerset Maugham."

I hung up.

But fancy J.'s being jealous.

•

Mondays belonged to the librarian. "He's *here!*" Cookie would scream as she climbed the stairs.

"Did you finish his last book already?"

"I like when he tells stories," she huffed. "That doesn't mean I have to read everything. I'm starting a nail polish collection and I'm having a hard time on the pinks."

He never failed to greet Sara's fetal pouch. "Good morning to Heather," to Sara's great delight, since she was becoming nauseatingly maternal.

"How's your little scholar?" I asked him as the girls thumbed the new books.

"Changing under my eyes. And the grandmother is furious. He was such a shy thing when I found him. Like me in a way, afraid of the terror who's raising him."

"You don't seem particularly shy to me."

"That, mademoiselle, is because I learned to read. She couldn't keep my spirit crippled. But she tried."

Gail had moved to the periphery of our conversation. "Your mother? You mean your mother?"

"Yes. I'm afraid so. Sometimes mothers are afraid to let go. Sometimes mothers welcome little cripples because they stay put. Always on call where their mothers can control them."

"You mean consciously Mothers who hate their children."

"No. Just because they need something they can't understand."

"But they mean well," said Gail, pulling at that lip.

"Hell is paved with good intentions," he answered her. "I learned that from a book also."

"Like Medea you mean. You have to understand Medea," said Gail, searching inward for some explanation. "She was hurt by Jason. So if she killed her children, you have to understand that she had suffered herself."

The librarian looked at me before he turned back to Gail. "Medea was a monster. Nobody escapes being hurt or disappointed in this world. Nobody is free of the whims of the gods. If you read your mythology you understand that well enough. Medea was mad to take out her disappointments on her children. There was no excuse for Medea." He waited to see how his customer would respond. "Keep reading. You'll find the book you need."

Gail considered his statement. "Can you bring me *Alice in Wonderland?*"

"Good. Did you know that *Alice* has a deeper symbolic meaning?"

"Naturally. Every ten-year-old knows that. I was just thinking about how Alice has always frightened me. I mean the general instability of her condition. She keeps falling and changing. She can never be certain of what reality is for her."

"But," said the librarian, raising a finger and smiling in his comforting way, "it never really frightens *her*, does it? I mean she takes the whole thing rather well."

He turned his smile to Sara, who had brought her crocheting over to sit near us. "What book shall I bring for Sara and Heather?"

Sara closed her eyes, put down her handwork, turned inward to seek her choice. "I want a book," she said solemnly, "bring me a book about a princess who tried too hard to hold her prince. She held too tight and he turned into a deer and ran off into the deep woods." She opened her eyes, took his hand in hers, pressed it against her cheek, "but please make the prince ride up in the last chapter and snatch her and the little princess and ride off with them. Find that book." She kissed his hand.

"Shall he come on a great white charger?" asked the librarian.

"He can come in a little VW bus with a sign on the back that says *love*." She released his hand and took up her crocheting but she did not turn to the window. She sighed and continued to make her booties or whatever little thing it was.

The librarian looked at her for a moment and then turned his attention to me. He touched my hand and he asked me, "And you? What book shall I bring you?"

The Black-shawled Abuela

It was on the morning of our librarian's Monday that Doris and the old secretary looked up from their huddled conversation and shared significant glances as I passed.

Nothing to be concerned about. I got a lot of significant glances from Doris. I could see her mouth working into a comment, but she was being careful about her phraseology. "I hope that you checked very thoroughly the kind of material your librarian brought into your classroom. You have not been vigilant."

"Vigilant," echoed the secretary.

I returned to the desk. "Vigilant about what?"

"You ought to be a judge of who is a proper instructor for our girls and who is not," said Doris. "A teacher should be observant."

"Observant of what, Doris?"

"Everybody is talking about it," said the old secretary.

"There is a perfectly good shelf of books upstairs," said Doris. "So let's say no more about it."

"About what!" I demanded, evidently raising my voice because Miss Rodriguiz came out of her office.

"Are you at it again? Hasn't anybody around here read Freud? This isn't the Middle Ages. Leave the poor man alone." She retreated. I heard her door slam.

"I want to know what's the matter with our librarian," I asked again. "He'll be here in an hour and I don't want him embarrassed."

"I don't expect he'll be here at all. If he does come our doors will be closed to him," said Doris. And then she clammed up. When Doris seals her jaws, the topic is dead. The secretary returned to her ivy.

Nurse Caulfield was just coming out of clinic as I reached the second floor landing. "What's going on with our librarian?" I asked her. "Have you heard anything?"

"Anything? I was just coming to look for you. I think it's a crying shame when a man hasn't a right to be what he wants without this puritanical society smacking him down. Just because a man has a hormonal imbalance."

"Who has what imbalance? Where did anyone get our librarian's medical history?"

"A man has a perfect right to any sex practices with another consenting male. That's my point of view. Of course with a boy it's another kettle of fish. But I don't believe a word of that. A man has a right to privacy without the whole world watching through his bedroom window. Everybody ought to take nurses' training. You'd be amazed at the peculiar sex practices of perfectly normal people."

"Are you implying that he's a homosexual? The man is married!"

"That's the trouble with our hypocritical society. To make a man live a lie! And why should he be kicked out of his job? It's perfect for his type. Did you know that some of them marry just to have children? Let's face it. Some lesbians make great teachers. They devote themselves, if you know what I mean."

.

Luckily first period went to the nutritionist so that I had a chance to get to a phone. I reached the Main Library.

"He's not in just now," I was told. "He's in the field."

"Simply in the field?" I asked. "Nothing more?"

"What more did you want?" she asked.

So I called J. I had difficulty in phrasing my question because I wasn't certain of what I wanted to ask him.

"Look, how can you determine if a man's a homosexual?"

"Get into bed with him. Anything else? I'm busy."

"Yes," I said against the pounding of my heart. "Have you ever had doubts about me? As a woman I mean?"

"Yes, I've had doubts about you. As a woman."

"How?" I demanded. "In what way?"

"As far as your hormones are concerned and as far as your ability to stimulate the normal male is concerned, you're a woman. But as far as your heart is concerned a steam bath wouldn't thaw you out."

He hung up.

Men are impossible.

You ask simple logical questions and you get emotional answers.

.

Cookie was the first to rush into my room, panting with exertion. "He's *not* a fruit!" she screamed. "If there's one thing I know in this world it's when a man's a fruit and not a fruit! That's my specialty."

Gail stormed in, visibly angry, perspiration dampening her forehead. She slammed a book on my desk. Something to do with Hammurabi's Code. "They have no right to persecute a gentle man. I'm going to write a denunciation. How do you spell *J'accuse*? I forgot my French!"

"Just leave it to your generation," said Sara bitterly, slumping into a chair. "A man can't do his own thing without everybody tearing him to bits. The minute they find a man full of love they try to destroy him."

"I like him," said Mary Lou. "I hope he doesn't do anything unnatural against God. God is very strict."

"I'm trying to *tell* you," screamed Cookie, "that it's not true! He's not a fag! He might be small but lots of small men are sexy! Ask me!"

"What if his wife hears this dumb talk and leaves him?" asked Sara angrily. "Maybe he's home right now without anybody to comfort him. No one should be alone. Animals wouldn't be that unloving to each other."

"Horses wouldn't," said Marlene.

"Dogs wouldn't," added Baby.

"Why is the world so unfeeling?" demanded Sara passionately. "If I didn't have Heather to love I think I would die. Why does it have to be like that?"

"Why indeed?" asked a voice from the doorway. Our librarian stood pale and shaken, his book bag dragging on the floor behind him. Doris was fast on his heels. He turned and in cold courtesy he asked her, "Madame, is there something you want of me? I have books to bring my ladies."

"Just wait until I make a call," said Doris in confusion. "Just wait here." She looked me a signal. "Just everybody wait right here!"

The moment she descended the stairs the girls pulled him inside and slammed the door. Helen dragged a chair and stuck it under the knob.

"Asylum!" heralded Gail. "You have asylum here! This is a place of religious devotion! Life is created here and we offer you our protection!"

"I thank you," he said wearily. "If anyone needs asylum I am he."

"He's so upset he's talking funny," said Helen.

The librarian dragged his foot toward my chair, fell into it. Sara came to his side, embraced him sympathetically.

"But what happened?" I asked him. "I've been trying all morning to make some sense out of these innuendoes."

"That's the whole of it. Inferences. Innuendoes. I'm the victim of a whispering campaign."

"I knew it!" cried Cookie. "I know when a man is a swish and not a swish. A man doesn't have to be enormous to be manful. I can always tell!"

He rose painfully from his chair, walked over to where she was standing. He took her puffy hand and kissed the back of it solemnly. "Thank you, Cookie. That's the first decent thing anyone has said to me all week."

"Me too," begged Baby, holding out her fat little hand.

"Someone sure must have it in for you," said Helen. "It happened to me once."

"I'm afraid somebody does. I'm the victim of a black-shawled abuela."

"An abooella!" said Cookie in horror. "Is it like the Mafia?"

"It's someone's grandmother," said Gail. "Is it a vendetta or a blood feud of some sort?"

"It's the grandmother of one of my students in Great Books. The boy was reading like mad and the old woman was furious because he came home late and started to question her about the Church. She called me an antichrist. She tried to get me fired, but she didn't have any grounds. So she just started to whisper."

"Lousy," said Helen. "I had this girl named Consuelo whisper about me. Don't let her get away with it."

"What can I do? I can't fight a shadow. I can't fight the wind. Suddenly all the black-shawled grandmothers are staring at me as I pass. They call my leg the curse of the devil. Because I'm an unnatural man."

"You're natural," said Baby consolingly.

"Why not get a lawyer?" I suggested. "You can't let them slander you. Have you lost your job?"

"Not at all. The library is very sympathetic. But nobody brings charges. The whole ugly thing is carried on behind shawls."

Doris banged on the door. "Open this up, please!"

"Don't let her in," said Helen. "This place is an asylum. Gail said so."

"Will your wife stick by you?" asked a concerned Sara. "I mean she won't let you down."

"She won't let me down, but without meaning to she watches me from the corner of her eye."

"I insist!" called Doris shrilly.

I removed the chair and stepped outside, closing the door behind me.

"What's going on in there?" demanded Doris. Slightly hysterical.

"Did you phone the library?"

"They said they knew nothing about it." She tried to reach behind me to open the door.

"Well, has it occurred to you that you might have been mistaken? That you might be doing a terrible injustice to an innocent man?"

Her firm resolve withered into indecision as she weighed my words. "Watch him," she cautioned. "Where there's smoke there's fire."

"Did you read that in your upstairs books, Doris?"

She searched her experience for a retort. I could see that she wanted to assume her responsibility but she didn't know what it was.

"I'll call Downtown," she decided finally.

Let her. Everything reported to Downtown had to go through channels. And all channels led to the Dead Sea. A perturbed Doris descended, leaving our librarian in the protective center of his ladies.

"There was this girl Consuelo," continued Helen. "I beat her up. Right in the classroom of juvenile hall. I knocked out two teeth. She'll have a sore mouth for a year. You ought to get someone to beat up this grandmother."

"Helen," I told her, "you can't fight violence with violence."

"Who says? You ought to see the space in her mouth. Let her whisper through that."

"I wouldn't even of come here," said Marlene, "except people were whispering about me."

"Who whispered?" asked Baby. "What did they say?"

"I don't know but my mother heard them."

"Look," said Sara, stroking his hands, "maybe you can just go to his grandmother with love and explain yourself. Bring her some flowers. I've seen these rough policemen smash into a house and we gave them flowers and herb tea and they left really happy for the first time in their lives. Some people have to learn about love."

"I'll ask my boyfriend in the Army," said Mary Lou. "The Army knows about everything."

"No army can fight a whisper," said the librarian. "I think I'll just pick up and move. We'll try another city. Anything to get away from this madness."

"Don't go away," pleaded Baby and Marlene. "We'll be your friend."

"I knew I had friends here. I just couldn't figure out where else to go. I was sitting in Joe's drinking coffee and they came in and stared."

"Don't pay any attention to it," counseled Sara. "Don't you

think they whisper about us when we walk to the drugstore?"

"Old crabs," said Cookie.

The conspirators were drawn together in common cause, mulling the nature of man's relationship to man. The gas pains forgotten. The backaches gone. I watched them from the edge of the group.

"We'll help you," said Cookie. "That's the least we can do. We'll write a letter to all the people in the neighborhood and tell them that the old lady is a rotten liar."

"Tell your mother to talk to that lady," said Marlene. "You should have heard what my mother said to that neighbor before I came."

"Alas, not my mother," he sighed. "She spends half her time bleaching her hair and the other half in Las Vegas. She wouldn't be a proper emissary."

"You're just talking and not *doing* anything," said Cookie in frustration. "Then *I'll* do it! It's the *least* a person can do for a friend." She pulled herself up to her full broad tragic height, the stance she had used in her brief theatrical career. "I'll tell everybody he's the father of my baby. Then they'll never call him a fag again! I'll tell everybody I knew him from before and he's a great lover!"

"You cluck!" laughed Helen.

"Don't call me that!" said Cookie. "Let's see you do something better!"

"It's a beautiful sacrifice," said the librarian gallantly. "I thank you. Sydney Carton's sacrifice was not more appreciated. But, Cookie, I'm afraid that it might upset my wife."

"She could be in on it. I could go in secret in the night with a veil and explain it to her."

"With that stomach," said Helen, "you'd have to wear a whole mile of mosquito netting."

"There is a solution," said Gail. "We'll fight deception with deception. We'll hire an old woman to act as your abuela. She can drag herself to the boy's grandmother and plead in tears for your reputation. And if that doesn't stop the whispering lies, she'll place a curse on the whole family. Like the House of Atreus."

"I'll chip in," said Cookie. "I'll sell my polish collection." Our librarian was laughing. "I mean it," said Cookie. "Nobody in the world has a collection like mine."

The conspirators were laughing. I suppose that I wasn't because I didn't logically see that there was anything to laugh about. His problem was unresolved. I wondered if he had tried the library's union or whether he might not have legal recourse if he could find witnesses to the slurs and accusations.

But Sara leaned over and kissed his cheek. "You see? When people love each other, things come out okay. It's only when they're not together that things go bad." Her laughter died when her words reached her own ears, registered in her own heart.

"Books!" called our librarian, reaching for his book bag. "Who's for a book about a poor man almost destroyed by whisperers?"

"How does it come out?" asked Sara.

"How does anything come out?" asked the gentle librarian. "Sometimes endings aren't clear. But I suppose that you can still enjoy the story."

"But it must come out," said Sara. "It has to." She was suddenly dead serious, a dead-serious, pregnant sixteen-year-old who rested her hands on her swelling belly. "If it doesn't come out," she said in such an unaffected voice that I scarcely recognized it, with such a flat expressionless face that it was hardly Sara, "if it doesn't come out," she repeated, "what the hell am I going to do?"

What Light from Yonder Window

GAIL AND SARA hailed me from the little visitors' room as I passed on my way to the office. Sara was sitting cross-legged on the sofa, making a fan on the cushion of what seemed to be money. She scooped up a handful of bills, waved them at me.

"Do you know what this is?" she asked spitefully.

"It looks like money. Unless it's counterfeit."

"Remember *Hamlet*," said Gail, looking sympathetically at Sara's anguished face. "Things are not what they seem."

"You're blind," said Sara shrilly. "It's love. Don't you know love when you see love?"

"She wrote her parents in Omaha," said Gail. "When she thought her hours were numbered. And this is their response."

"Their usual response," said Sara. "A handful of love. And do you think they asked one word about my baby? About my almost dead baby?"

That was a rhetorical question. Clearly. But I sensed her deep distress.

"I'll tell you what I'm going to do with this love," she said, gathering it in a fistful and starting for the stairs, waving it over her head. "I'm going to make a collage. Like a green forest. And I'm going to cut this up for leaves."

"What's happening here?" asked Doris, stepping out of the office.

"I'm getting ready to cut this up for my collage," she announced again to the girls who drifted out of breakfast.

"Indeed you can't," said Doris. "It's illegal to destroy money. It's like defacing the flag."

"Whose flag! It's my money. I can destroy it if I want to!"

"Don't," pleaded Cookie, pushing around Doris. "I'm going to the drugstore. They have a whole new line, toward the fuchsia. You can come with me."

"Think of the good that money will do," said Doris. "Think of the poor children."

"Think of the harm it's done already to some poor children," said Sara. She headed toward the stairs.

Miss Rodriguiz had stepped out of her office, stood with me and watched Sara climb, Gail fast behind her. "Is she at it again?" asked Miss Rodriguiz as she made her clipboard notes.

Those notes made me furious. As if a word scribbled on a paper in a firm hand made it necessarily valid. And what did she mean *at it again?* If she were any sort of psychologist she could see that the distress on Sara's face was genuine.

"I'd be upset too if I wrote home asking for love and got money instead."

"And you're getting sucked in again. I thought you learned your lesson."

And not just the notes. The tone of her voice — as if her self-assurance made her words valid.

"Is it just possible," I asked her, with perhaps a hint of impatience, "that Sara really thought she'd killed her baby? That her histrionics were real? And you saw the money. You saw the callous response to her appeal."

"Why do you always have to blame someone?" Her voice mocked me. I'm sure it did.

"Why not? If the fault is there."

"Her parents hadn't heard from her in over a year. Then in a fit of self-pity she mails them a card. 'Congratulations. You're about to be grandparents.' They sent her what they thought was protection and food and shelter. That was the only love they could send in the framework of the situation as they knew it. So are you sure you want to blame them?"

"You see the way she always takes off on what she calls *my* generation. She's been terribly hurt."

"Don't get paranoid. The first thing you have to learn about teaching at Huntington House is not to get paranoid. It isn't *your* generation, is it? Just because she calls it that way? Teen-agers are very emotional and pregnant teen-agers are worse. I don't blame anybody. I'm a sociologist. I observe and I note and I try to offer alternatives. And if I were you I'd stick to my poetry and leave the psychoanalysis to the ones who are equipped to handle it."

I stamped upstairs. I turned once to see her smiling up at me. Supercilious. She was the type who probably swam like a fish.

My first-period girls held a rousing discussion about why the boy in *The Yearling* needed a deer. Two of them made pale comments and one answered a direct question in a substandard fragment sentence. I had to take a cup of tea before second.

When I returned the girls had already gathered. Sara had her money spread out before her on the table, moving the bills about with her finger like dry leaves.

"They cut down trees to make this!" she accused. "Do you know how long it takes nature to grow a redwood tree?"

"How long?" asked Marlene.

"I don't think they make money out of redwood," I said.

"That's all you know about it," she muttered.

"I'd like to get back to *The Bridge of San Luis Rey*. Remember that the little group was crossing a deep chasm on a rope bridge and the rope bridge broke, hurling them to their death in the canyon below."

"Why can't we have a spelling test?" wailed Cookie. "Instead of all these people having problems."

"You want to have a spelling test? Instead of a story?"

"Sure because in spelling tests you study it and you take it and you get your grade and you get your credit and it's over. You don't have to think about it for a year."

"That's right," agreed Helen. "I always get A's on spelling tests."

"If you get A's on spelling tests why do you misspell so many words on your essays?"

"Because," she said, clutching her letter, "I said spelling *tests*, not regular spelling. Don't you know anything?"

They sank back to their lethargy. No. I didn't know anything. Really what difference did it make at all? If Gail knew *Julius Caesar* iamb by iamb what difference did it make when her mother's spirit came over her like a pall? If all the eggs in the world were hatched one by one in front of their eyes would it affect how they felt the next time a blue-eyed David reached out his warm hand?

And so I didn't bother to draw them back from their daydreams. And I was rather submerged in mine.

J. had accused me outright of being insensitive. It was a lie. If anything I was *more* sensitive. I was easily hurt. And he knew it. And to make accusations was callous and unfeeling. You don't get held up in water by an attacking shark.

When I came to the surface I found most of them reading quietly. At least that. Sara rested her head on the pile of money, scratching at the table with her fingers. I suppose I heard the sound a couple of times before I actually listened to it.

A male voice from outside called, "Heloise!"

Gail looked up from her book, winced, returned to her reading.

"Heloise!" it called again.

"Someone is calling," said Sara, lifting her head from her money bed and focusing her eyes. "Who's Heloise?"

Chairs were pushed away from tables and the group moved toward the dusty windows. I moved with them, but I noticed that Gail had remained at her desk.

"Did you hear it?" she asked me. "I thought . . ." She passed a hand across her mouth.

"It's a tall skinny boy," Cookie announced. "We don't have any Heloise in the house."

"Roxanne!" he called. "Come down! A message along the vines! Please!"

"He's calling me," said Gail. "He found me." She trembled, looked to me, to the window, but she didn't move.

"He's goofy," said Helen. "Is he the guy from the nuthouse?"

I joined the girls at the window. The boy stood across the street, leaning against a telephone pole, looking up at the building. The damp of the morning had coalesced into a faint drizzle. He wore a T-shirt, no sweater. He waved his arm.

"Juliet!" he pleaded.

"It's a good thing you didn't give him your real name," said Cookie. "If you don't know a man you should always give him a phony name."

"I was Juliet," said Gail, without moving any further toward the source of the sound. "I was Roxanne."

"Tell him you're here," called Sara from the window. "Don't just let him stand there in the cold. Wave to him."

"I can't." Gail gripped the edge of her table with tense fingers.

"Why not?" asked Sara urgently. "Don't you love him?"

"I can't," she repeated without emotion. No note in her voice that she was concerned about the boy in the street. Yet her arms were rigid and her face was bathed in sweat. I didn't want a miscarriage in the classroom. She frightened me.

"Just sit there," I cautioned her. "I'll call Nurse Caulfield."

"She doesn't have to sit," said Sara. "She needs to come to the window and tell her love she's up here."

Miss Rodriguez rushed into the room just as he called again, a passionate plea. "Violetta! Come down!"

"We don't know how he found you but just cool it, Gail. Okay? They're coming for him. Keep an eye on her," she cautioned me. She checked to see Gail's condition and rushed out.

"Who's coming?" demanded Sara.

"Why are they coming?" asked Gail, holding on to the edge of her table for support. "He's not hurting anyone. He's just sick."

She managed to rise and stumble to the window. Cookie had cranked the ancient gears and the window was open a hand's span. There was Cara's dove ledge, a few feathers, and down in the street a tall, skinny, shivering poet wailing, "Come down."

"She's here!" yelled Cookie. "Up here!"

He turned his face in our direction. "Gail!" he called. "I need you!"

Gail was mesmerized, holding her stomach, sweating, dazed. I watched her as I had been ordered, but I didn't know what else to do.

"Why are they coming?" Sara asked again. "Why do they come after the ones who don't hurt people? They!" she accused with rancor.

"Come down, Gail!" he begged. "Hold my hand! I'm dying!"

"Is he dying?" asked Cookie. "Is this his last request before he dies of a terrible sickness?"

"A death of the spirit," said Gail faintly. "A beautiful spirit and nobody but I could see it. I am his eyes. They blinded him."

"He should have a white cane," said Cookie sympathetically.

"Go to him," pleaded Sara. "He needs you. If I only had the

chance," she said desperately, "I'd walk barefooted. I'd run naked. If I had the chance. Go on, Gail!"

"Just stay where you are until the nurse comes," I warned her. She was pale, almost to fainting.

"I want to go but my feet won't work. Who has the Medusa's head? I'm turned to stone."

"Look how funny she is," said Mary Lou. "Better say a Hail Mary. She might be getting a punishment."

"You're just frightened," said Sara. "Everybody's frightened. I'm frightened. But don't let it stop you. Go down to him!"

"He raped me. He tried to kill me."

"Did he?" asked Cookie with interest. "Were you raped?"

"My mother said I was. It was a lie. We only joined together to leave this nightmare world."

"Then *go* to him," begged Sara.

Gail looked down finally. "Harvey!" she called with all her strength.

"Hurry!" he called. "Please hurry!"

"I can't walk," moaned Gail. "My feet won't move."

Sara took her by the arm. "Yes, you can."

Slowly they both moved toward the door and I moved to stop them.

"He's gone," announced Baby from the window. "They took him away in a car."

"Is he gone?" asked Gail, almost in a monotone.

"It just drove up and took him," said Baby sadly.

I went to the window. The street was empty. Gray, wet, oppressive, and empty.

Gail collapsed against Sara and wept. "Il pleure dans mon coeur comme il pleut dans la ville," she sobbed.

Sara stroked her head. "You remember your French. You finally remembered."

"Is it French?" Gail wept.

"And you were going," said Sara. "You started to go. If they hadn't taken him, the rotten bastards, you would have been down there."

"Was I going?" she begged.

"Sure," comforted Cookie. "Look where you were and look where you are."

"Dominus vobiscum," wept Gail. "Miseracordia."

"You can say that again," said Mary Lou.

"I think I was going," said Gail, wiping her eyes with the back of her hand. "I have to do things faster. That was always my problem. I never did things fast enough." She fastened her eyes on Sara. "Sara will do it. Sara will descend the mountains with her babe, throwing rocks at the Philistines, and she'll march across the land suckling her babe. She'll do it for me."

She walked unsteadily back to her seat, fell into it, opened her book, began to read as if she had never been interrupted. The girls returned to their places.

"Open to Chapter Four," was all I could suggest.

"That's all your generation wants us to do," muttered Sara as she opened her book. "Isolate ourselves from pain and feeling." She spoke to silence. "You have to feel pain sometimes," she said, her head still bent toward the book she wasn't reading, the green currency still spread out beneath it. "At least he came." She pushed her book aside, muffled her face in her arms.

Silence. Only the sounds of doves which had the confidence to return to their ledge. Baby and Marlene returned to *Teen Tales*. I corrected a few papers, listlessly making little notes on the bottom about how interesting the ideas were but why didn't the author make an attempt to organize them. Such things. Doris poked her head into the quiet room, surveyed the heads bent over books.

"Lovely," she said in a hoarse whisper. "Lovely control. Good teaching."

In the ensuing silence only Sara's eyes rose to meet mine. "They're out to get us," she said softly, "to lock us all away from the woods and the water." She folded her money neatly and stuffed it into a pocket. "They're very strong. But they *won't* get us." She addressed her baby. "Not us, Heather." She looked to me for reinforcement. I tried not to meet her eyes. I was slipping into a morass.

Black Is the Color

DORIS ACTUALLY SMILED at me as I entered the office. That in itself was depressing.

"Yes," she said. "I think you're coming to understand the nature of teaching at Huntington House. Work that gives them a chance for quiet reflection. Book reports are grand," she added in a confidential tone, as if she were offering me a state secret.

I nodded in an ambiguous response. I wasn't in the mood to wrangle.

"And I've made you the Senior Class sponsor," she said cheerily.

"Why does the Senior Class need a sponsor?"

"To plan the graduation and chaperone the swimming party."

"*What* swimming party?"

"The swimming party to which we have been invited by a lovely and generous woman from Pasadena who owns a gracious home and a heated pool."

"What do you *mean* swimming party! Who's going to let a bunch of pregnant girls go swimming? With their problems!"

"I thought you would enjoy the assignment," she said with what I am *sure* was a touch of amusement. I had underestimated Doris. "The summer seniors always have a swimming party. And everybody has problems," she chided. "We don't need to dwell on them, do we? We ought to learn to think positive."

"Is that what you do, Doris? Do you always think positive?"

"If we would all think positive the world would be a brighter place."

"How do you expect me to chaperone a swimming party? I don't know how to swim."

"There's nothing to be nervous about," she said with a hint, I thought, of faint derision. "Nurse Caulfield will join you. She swims exceedingly well."

Definitely I had underestimated Doris.

"And are you seriously suggesting that we have a formal graduation from a maternity home? What sort of pictures will they have for the family album."

"Your negativism is not productive," said Doris, screwing up her mouth.

"The oceans are polluted, Doris, and the air is foul and the people of the world are consuming themselves in war. Give me one thing to think positive about!"

"Where there is life there is hope," stated Doris unequivocally, emphasizing the word *hope* with a lyrical upswing.

"Doris, tell me how to build hope on a false premise. These girls are getting ready to deliver babies which for the most part will be given away. Who is going to leave here happier and more fulfilled?"

"Why don't you give your class a little Emerson? That lovely poem about the chambered nautilus. How each little chamber grows into the new chambers of the spirit."

I wasn't in the mood for a little Emerson. "What do pregnant girls wear to a swimming party?"

"Bathing suits."

"And what if a girl drowns or gets dragged under by her weight? Or if she goes into labor in the water?"

I remembered *Moby Dick* and the detailed descriptions of little whales being born and the umbilical cords becoming tangled in the lines.

She thought I was being funny. I detected a smile. Or a smirk.

.

I told them all second period.

"I'm the sponsor of the Senior Class."

"Rah rah," said Sara. "When do we start making pompons?"

"Can we make pompons?" asked Marlene enthusiastically.

"And the Senior Class has been invited by a gracious lady to a lovely luncheon and a swimming party."

"Heather and I won't go," said Sara. And more softly, "But we'll go to the ocean this summer and I'll hold her and dip her little feet in the water. She'll be a little mermaid."

Marlene and Baby cooed like doves. "Tell us about Heather," they begged. "Tell us about the woods and all that."

"I'll wear my new bikini!" screamed Cookie. "I bought it to wear in Lake Arrowhead and I never wore it."

"What did you wear in Lake Arrowhead?" asked Helen.

"Don't ask," said Cookie.

"Water is good therapy," said Gail. "If it's warm. Like a baptism."

"Then I'll go," said Sara impulsively, "but I won't go so deep this time. Heather and I will just be a little in the water." She lifted her arms and dropped imaginary sheets of water on her upturned face. "Heather will get the feel of it. Because when we're back in the woods I'm going to make a little raft for her out of branches tied together and I know this peaceful dammed-up place and Heather and I will just drift lazy under the sun."

"I wish I could do that," said Baby awefully. "But my mother would never let me."

"Heather and I aren't going to be afraid. That's the way I'm going to make her."

"I haven't got a bathing suit," said Baby. "Can I swim in my shorts and a blouse?"

"I swim naked," announced Sara. "That's the only way to swim. We used to run naked under waterfalls. With all sorts of people we didn't actually know. That was so beautiful." She gave me the old cold eye. "I suppose that your generation would be shocked."

"I don't think you're allowed to swim naked in Pasadena."

"Try and stop us. Heather and I will both swim naked and when I get out of the water I'll wear the African dashiki Wanda gave me before she went over. I bet they'll love that in Pasadena."

A voice cut through the room. "It's not your style, honey. You would look phony in a dashiki with all that yellow hair. That is where the black girl has it all over the white girl. You look phony in our clothes and we look grand in yours."

The speaker posed languidly in the doorway, a full, doe-eyed imperious Queen of Sheba. She entered slowly and deliberately, walking casually between the chairs as if her handmaidens were carrying her train. She dropped a registration card on my desk. Rona L. She was a senior.

I welcomed her. "This is Rona who's come to join our class. Just in time for the swimming party."

"Hi!" called Sara generously. In spite of the opening. "Come on and sit down."

"I don't need to be invited to sit down," said Rona, walking dramatically across the room to find a lone seat. "The chair is as much mine as it is yours. So I don't need an invitation to take what's mine, do I."

Sara winced, relaxed, smiled again. Stung by the rebuff and

ready to forgive. A thing which I found hard to understand. Rona seated herself, tall and imperturbable, but I saw that she curled her fingers to hide the close-bitten nails.

"I suppose that you're reading white writers in this class," she said, in my general direction but never meeting my eyes. "If you don't have a list of black writers I'll bring you one. Some white teachers don't know black writers. So don't be too proud to accept a little guidance. We all have room for improvement. Don't we?"

All this delivered for the benefit of the class. I was about to be angry. I could feel it in my gorge. And it evidently reflected on my face. Sara picked it up with the radar of "her" generation.

"Don't blame *her*," accused Sara. "The way your generation has put down her and her sisters."

"Don't fight my battles, honey," said Rona, returning acid for Sara's open smile. "I can take care of myself."

A rebuffed Sara fell back in chagrin, weighing her sister's remarks.

"Is it unanimous?" I asked, trying to break the mood. "Do we all want to go swimming?"

"*We* want to go," said Cookie, "but some people can butt out! If they don't know when people are just trying to be friendly."

"Honey, I choose my friends carefully," said Rona.

I made a mental note to consult Miss Rodriguiz. I made a mental note to think about Sara, why she had been twice slapped and yet continued to offer her love.

"Then can we please get back to *The Bridge of San Luis Rey*."

"Don't they have any decent help in this house?" asked Rona, as if the whole class were interested. "I had to rearrange a whole closet to put my things away."

"We don't have help here, Rona," said Sara, up for a third try. Tenacious. Smiling. "This is a sort of commune. We all share the work and we all share the house. So we don't mind pitching in. That's the way the whole world should be."

"Thanks, honey, but I don't need to share a room with somebody who slops up with a bunch of filthy lipsticks."

Cookie almost overturned the table. "Are you in my room? They never told me someone was coming into my room! Did you touch my lipstick color wheel?"

"Who would want to touch that disgusting thing? I just moved your dirty shoes."

"If you ruin my things," screamed Cookie, "I'm not going to be responsible!"

"Don't threaten me, you white cow."

Helen rose slowly from her chair. "You're asking for it!"

"That's enough!" I ordered them. I hate violence. "If there are hard feelings get them out on paper."

Gail had already withdrawn behind her book. Baby and Marlene huddled in their corner. Mary Lou was fingering her little crucifix.

"No," protested Sara. Still hanging on. "We don't want to put our feelings on paper. That's what your generation would do," but the glance she threw me had no hint of reproach. "Rona's new here. She just doesn't understand Huntington House. But we want her to know that we're not mad and we're her sisters."

"Screw her," said Helen. "You be her sister."

Rona turned her nailless fingers inward, turned her eyes to the ceiling, feigning nonchalance but her eyes brimmed with tears.

"That's what I want to teach Heather," continued Sara. "I want her to know what love is. It can be a gentle world, like the animals. There'll be lots of people where we'll live, all colors of people. And I'll make my baby a cradle out of branches and rock her in the forest while the little animals sit close by. And when she cries it won't matter if I'm there or not because all her brothers and sisters will pick her up and love her just the same."

Baby and Marlene were mesmerized. For a moment the picture fascinated me. But Rona cut the room with her harsh forced laughter.

"What's that, honey? A story by Walt Disney? Who's taking this fairy-tale baby back to what woods?"

She had found a soft spot and she cut in, leveling her eyes on Sara.

"The father of my baby is coming," said Sara helplessly, enmeshed in her own tale. "He is coming in a little VW bus to take us back to the woods where Heather was first made. We made her there in the forest just the way you plant a seed in the earth."

"And he's coming back to fetch you," mocked Rona disdainfully.

"Yes!" said Baby. "To make the cradle!"

"He'll be there!" said Helen threateningly.

"God will make him," said Mary Lou. "I lit a candle."

Rona smiled in satisfaction. "Honey, that's what makes us truly equal. The black boys and the white boys, they all hand out the same shit."

Sara half rose, wounded by the attack.

"Rona, don't!" I called involuntarily. Rona sank back and Sara sank back. A crushed Sara. She could say no other word. Once she started to speak but a little animal sound came from her and then she was silent.

"He'll come," whimpered Baby.

"Enough!" I said. "I want you to go to your rooms and read. Rona, you stay here."

"I'll stay if it pleases me," said Rona. The class filed out angrily, surrounding Sara with their sympathy.

"Give it to her," said Helen fiercely as she walked by. Sara gave me a defenseless glance and walked out. I wanted to follow her and comfort her. But she had trapped herself. That was the penalty of fantasy. And it proved my point. But it hurt me to see her.

Rona sat, not looking at me. I evaluated her. Actually, a stunning girl, graceful, pregnant, with a palpable roundness.

"Look, Rona. We need to talk over what happened."

"Why? What happened?" she asked in a flat uninterested voice.

"Sara tried to tell you. This is a new environment. It takes time to become part of the group."

"I don't want to be a part of any group. I am Rona. I am an individual."

"I don't want to take away any part of your individuality, but you have to consider the feelings of the other members of the class."

"Why are you lecturing me?" she asked. "I didn't hear you lecture that cow!"

"You provoked her."

"No, I did not provoke anyone."

"Rona, I heard you."

"You can think what you want to think. That's your problem, isn't it."

"Look Rona, try to recall . . ."

"Honey, I recall everything. White people just look for ways to criticize black people. We all know that."

"Look Rona . . ."

"And don't raise your voice to me," she warned softly. "It's our taxes pays your salary. So honey, remember your place."

.

"Tea is as bad as coffee," said J. "No wonder you're not sleeping. You're hitting that tea bag pretty hard."

"How do you know I'm drinking tea?"

"I hear your teeth against the cup. Don't let it get to you. You're making progress."

"You've got your directions mixed. Progress means forward. I'm on a treadmill. I dream about cat imagery and stepfathers and water breaking. And I can't finish one whole unit to anyone's satisfaction."

"Trudge awhile. It won't hurt you."

"I'm depressed and you're happy. It indicates exactly how you feel about me, doesn't it."

"It does if you read the signs. You read symbols well enough but can you read signs?"

"Go to hell," I said. "I have to chaperone my senior girls at a swimming party in Pasadena."

He actually laughed.

"And I've got Rona."

"What's rona? A female condition?"

"A social condition. Did anyone ever tell you you were cold and unsympathetic? You accuse other people of being cold and you are the coldest."

"Wonderful! Good! You always ask for logic. Now you're asking for warmth and sympathy. Kid, that's beautiful."

"I don't want your rotten warmth and I don't want your rotten sympathy. I'm not letting myself count on anyone who'd let you drown when you were just learning to swim! I can take care of myself. If you let yourself count on anyone's warmth and sympathy it makes you too vulnerable. I learned that lesson from Sara today."

"And if you count on no one," he said softly, "you're alone, aren't you."

My tea was cold.

"I'll tell you what's the matter with you," I said. "You're just jealous of my independence. You like to see me insecure because it makes me dependent and it makes you superior. Admit it."

"I admit it," he said.

I hung up.

The Swimming Party

It wasn't the swimming party that upset me. It was the prospect of taking a carload of pregnant girls on the freeway. I hate the freeway. All tumult and aggressive drivers honking when one simply wants to keep a sane pace.

"Don't be nervous," said Doris solicitously as we routed our course in red ink on a freeway map.

"It's overcast," I protested. "The girls will catch cold."

"It will be warm in a half hour," said Doris. "I checked the report with the Weather Bureau." As if the Weather Bureau was the Oracle of Delphi.

And I wasn't nervous. I simply had a foreboding of impending disaster. Nurse Caulfield bounced around athletically. "Are you taking your suit or are you wearing it under your pants?" she asked.

"I probably won't swim," I answered, simply not wishing to discuss the matter further.

"Don't let the curse stop you," she said. "I'll fix you up."

"She doesn't swim," announced Doris, with consummate satisfaction, I thought. What a fool I was to have released that information to her.

"I'll check the girls," I said. I supposed that a chaperone was obliged to check the girls. At least that. If any of them drowned, there wasn't a thing I could do.

It was Sara and Rona who concerned me. The Senior Class was gathering in the little visitors' room. Sara sat with Gail on the tacky plastic sofa, eyes closed, loose hair falling across her face. Only by the forlorn angle of her shoulders could I judge her mood. Her feet were propped against the knapsack on the floor. Marlene and Baby sat together, each holding a portion of the top of a large paper bag. Helen squatted on the floor, as best she could squat with that overhanging stomach. Her dungarees were entirely unbuttoned but a man's work blouse covered almost all of the opening. Mary Lou wore her party hair, a huge coil piled high and solidly lacquered. No Cookie. No Rona.

"Mary Lou, how are you going to swim with such fancy hair?"

"I swim with my head out," she said.

When Rona entered, the eyes that greeted her were filled with rancor. Except for Sara's, which were ambiguously covered by her thick hair.

Baby's eyes were all sympathy for Sara. She and Marlene moved protectively to sit at Sara's feet. Baby moved her lips, trying to find words that would keep Heather safe. "Heather is going for a swim so she'll really be used to water when she comes." Rona did not respond. She merely lowered herself into a corner seat and averted her eyes. Sara said nothing.

"Heather's father was an Aquarius," continued Baby, "so Heather will probably swim before she can walk."

Rona turned her face slowly toward Sara, not Baby. "I expect he is a better runner than he is a swimmer."

Only Cookie and her large suitcase diffused the general anger that flashed toward Rona. "Why are you bringing such a big suitcase?" I asked her, relieved by the interruption.

"My things. I have to take my things for after the swim."

"Hey, it's not a three-day weekend," called Nurse Caulfield from the doorway. "You'll fill up the whole car."

"Then maybe *some* people will stay behind," said Cookie tartly, not looking at Rona.

"Let's go!" said Nurse Caulfield, with what I thought was unnecessary ebullience. It was a Senior Picnic, after all, and not a football game. "I'll take the little ones with me and Rona. Rona's not swimming either, are you, Rony? Maybe you and Rona can dangle together."

The thought of dangling with Rona was appalling.

Doris was waiting to bid us farewell as we trooped through the office. "Is there anything else you need to know?" she asked snidely.

"Yes. What shall I do if someone goes into labor on the free way?"

Nurse Caulfield thought that very funny. I didn't appreciate her levity. I was dead serious. "Just pull over to the side and call a policeman," she laughed.

"And be sure to thank the hostess," said Doris.

"I'm not a savage!" I answered savagely.

"Just relax and enjoy yourself," she advised me. "Don't be so tense. You ought to take swimming lessons."

It satisfied me to hear her say it. Because I didn't like Doris. And now I knew that I didn't have to feel guilty about it.

My station wagon was parked in the driveway in front of Nurse Caulfield's sporty little coupé. The wagon was already stuffed with Cookie's suitcase. The others piled their gear around it. I noticed that Sara kept her eyes on her knapsack and away from the road or the driveway or the parking lot, which did not contain any evidence of a VW bus. She and Gail piled into the front seat. The others climbed into the back, adjusting and re-adjusting their weighty bodies. The sun was starting to break through the clouds. If we didn't get killed on the freeway it might be a nice day.

"Let's drown Rona," said Helen, as I climbed behind the wheel.

"It's a mortal sin," said Mary Lou. "Can we make her go in with a full stomach and drown herself?"

Sara slumped against the car window, eyes closed, face pressed against the cool glass. Gail turned to her from time to time with concern.

"I'm leaving!" shouted Nurse Caulfield, and with an unnecessary burst of speed she scooped back and shot off down the street.

I turned to check the condition of my passengers. "Can you put Cookie's suitcase on its side? It's obscuring my rear vision. Is everybody ready?"

"We're not going west in a Conestoga wagon," said Sara, her first words of the morning. And rather petulant. That was all right. The light of reality is very sharp.

I pulled out of the driveway onto the street, made my way toward the freeway, wondering how best to control a car filled with pregnant women.

"Why are we going so slow?" asked Helen. "We'll miss lunch."

"Is everyone feeling all right?"

"I'm rolling down the window," said Sara.

"Why? What's wrong?"

"Nothing's wrong. I'm just rolling down the window. Your generation likes to be boxed and airless. I want to breathe."

She was all right. Slowly I headed toward the freeway on-ramp. The ramp was the worst of it. Cars whizzed by at extraordinary speeds. I waited until the lane was absolutely clear, ignoring the honking vehicles behind me. And slowly I proceeded. Little conversation. I drove carefully, following the white line of my lane. In general they seemed to be content to be traveling. And we moved along in peace.

"Oohhh!" moaned Cookie.

"What!" I cried, involuntarily turning around.

"Careful!" screamed Helen. "Don't turn around when you're on the freeway! Do you want to kill us?"

"Who moaned? What happened?"

"I broke a fingernail," said Cookie. "Now I have a stumpy hand just like that rotten Rona's."

"Let's drown her," suggested Helen again.

"Just leave her alone," said Sara. "Can't we go faster! God, I forgot what it feels like to go!"

"Don't bounce," said Gail. "It's too tight. I get claustrophobia if I'm squeezed."

"Let's never stop," said Sara. "Let's keep going until we hit the redwoods. I want the smell of pine needles to filter into my blood and flow into Heather."

Heather was revived. And we were headed not toward pine needles but toward Pasadena and Rona. This was going to be a great outing.

"Why do we have to have that dumb suitcase in the back?" asked Helen. "How come you needed a whole suitcase for a bikini and a towel?"

"I took my robe for after the swim."

"That's a big suitcase for a robe and a suit."

"I took my hair things for when my hair gets wet."

"All those curlers?" asked Helen. "You took your whole bag of curlers?"

"I took my dryer," said Cookie.

"You took a dryer to a swimming party?" I yelled back to her.

"Let's drown Rona," said Helen again. "She gives me a pain in the ass."

We arrived to find Nurse Caulfield and the others already lounging on the grassy lawn of what appeared to be a mansion.

Sara surveyed the manicured grounds with a critical eye.

"Excess baggage," she said. "What else does a person need but a sleeping bag and a stove and a couple of pots."

"A cradle made out of leafy boughs," said Rona.

"Rona, stop it," I warned her.

"Then tell *her* to cut it out," said Rona imperiously.

I wanted to buffer Sara's anger. But she wasn't angry. Only hurt, almost to tears, by the attack. I hoped she would not cry. Tears were foolish. They made her vulnerable. And they embarrassed me.

There was no further comment. We had been spotted by the generous and gracious Pasadena lady who stood at her open front door calling, "Welcome Seniors! Welcome all!"

I led the procession up the rose-lined path. The handsome gray-haired mistress of the manor smiled us in.

"How lovely of you to have us," I said in Doris's voice.

As we filed past her into the formal entry, Rona handed her hostess a little overnight case. "Just put it anywhere, honey," she commanded.

"Rony!" warned Nurse Caulfield.

"Make yourselves at home," said a perplexed but smiling hostess. "Luncheon is served whenever you are ready."

The girls lingered in the entry, awed by the Oriental paper and the mirrored walls, the vases of flowers, the heavy tapestries of the living room which we could see through an archway, the crystal of the chandeliers of the dining room to our right.

I could see several other ladies, elegantly arrayed, beautifully coifed, looking at the bellies. One rushed up and took Cookie's suitcase. "Let me help you," she offered. "That's too much to carry in your . . ." she floundered before she added, "condition."

"Thank you," said Cookie graciously. "Watch out for my make-up mirror."

"Let's eat, gals," said Nurse Caulfield from the dining room where she was keeping an eye on Rona. "We have to wait at least a half hour before swimming and the sun is already out."

Sara had made a fast survey of the rest of the house. "Ridiculous," she whispered to me. "I don't think that they ever sit on the chairs. But the *flowers* are real." She dragged me after her into the living room. Flowers in and out of season. Vases and containers of roses and carnations and chrysanthemums. Sara flitted from flower to flower, but the lithe bee was weighted. Sara was pregnant to bursting. I had not realized how pregnant until that moment as I watched her try to recapture what she had felt for flowers in her forest days. I saw her rummage in her pocket, find a rubber band, and reach up to tie back her hair. Her face was puffy. And flushed. I thought for some reason of Hester Prynne in *The Scarlet Letter*, the lovely auburn tresses of Hester after she and the baby were spurned by the community, the stern cap she wore to cover that hair, all tucked up under the confines of starched linen.

"Do you feel all right, Sara?" I asked her as she bent over a particularly long and graceful rose. She looked up at me, no rancor, no biting comment, just a sort of faint gesture of submission.

"I want Heather to know every single flower," she said, but I think she realized that she could not speak of Heather to me. When the portrait of the fat baby in the field of flowers reached out to me it dissipated, faded. And in a way I was sorry.

"I'm okay," she said. "Let's eat."

The tables rested under a magnificent chandelier. The casseroles and the service were obviously silver, the linen rich and fresh, the mixtures in their china dishes creamed and thick. Pasadena ladies hovered nervously behind the tables, lifting dish covers, offering rolls. There were seats only for the guests. The ladies were not dining with us. In silk and pearls they served corn bread and something with shrimp and little spiced apples, smiling at the girls like rich waitresses in some bizarre cafeteria.

Rona was the first to take a plate. She inspected the surface, rubbed it with her finger to remove some imaginary speck, looked into the casseroles that the ladies offered for her inspection.

"Awfully starchy," she sniffed, to the dismay of her hostess.

Sara took up a plate. "Making food for people is a real love thing," she announced, "and I thank you for it." She helped herself generously from each dish.

Rona had taken a dab of this and that and retired silently to the far end of the table. Sara chose a seat near her so that their eyes met obliquely. While the other girls laughed and bantered, Sara and Rona eyed each other silently. Sara's eyes asked questions. Rona's did not answer. But still it was a confrontation.

They all sunned themselves at poolside while Nurse Caulfield and I lingered over our tea and coffee. "What's the matter with Rona?" I asked her. "If she doesn't start something this afternoon it will be a miracle."

"Rona? She's okay. She's my buddy. Just a little under the weather. I told her to take it easy."

"She's a masochist. She goes out of her way to make enemies. Notice the way she baits Sara, and Sara is just trying to be friendly."

"Rona's just scared. Like the rest of them."

Through the glass doors we watched the girls beginning to undress. And the hostesses, glued to the windows, open-mouthed, watched them too.

A fantastic study in protuberances. Cookie pulled off her tent dress and there indeed was her new bikini. If you could make it out in the folds of flesh. Her pendulous breasts dragged the top down to the hump of her stomach. The bottom was a thread underneath the shelflike, taut belly from which her navel protruded.

"Do you like my suit?" she called to us through the open doors. We waved our approval.

Sara pulled off her smock. She was not naked. Her scanty suit stretched under the tight pouch that was Heather, visible evidence that there actually was a boy in a VW bus. She rubbed the belly lovingly.

"Heather moved her foot!" she laughed. "Heather is getting ready for her swim."

"Heather's going swimming first!" screeched Baby from the edge of the pool.

"That's right," called Rona from a seat at poolside. "You dip that baby in the cool stream. I can hear her daddy's bus in the driveway now. Have a quick dip before he comes, honey."

Sara dived neatly off the side, cut the water, came up with her wet hair in her face, paddled for a moment watching Rona. Then she laughed, tumbled over and over in the water like a fat dolphin.

Cookie lumbered over to the shallow side, lowered herself step by step until half her belly was submerged. She had found her level. She splashed herself in the warm water.

Mary Lou was swimming the length of the pool with her entire head out of water. Gail had appropriated one corner, on her back, holding the two sides with her hands, letting her feet drift, eyes closed in inner peace. Baby and Marlene splashed gleefully.

Only Rona did not swim. Nurse Caulfield and I joined her. She reclined in a wicker chair, hitting the wicker table beside her with the flat of her hand.

"Look, Rony," said Nurse Caulfield, squatting beside her, "are you feeling okay? You're acting rotten. I only wanted you to come because you were so low and I thought a party would cheer you up." She took Rona's hand. To my surprise Rona allowed her hand to be taken.

"I have a splitting headache," she complained, a nail-bitten hand to her forehead.

"Got something for you in the car," said Nurse Caulfield. "Have it here in a sec . . . Watch things," she called to me as she left.

Of course I'd watch things. I was the chaperone, wasn't I? But what I was chaperoning was a bunch of swimming conspirators, all bent on getting Rona. No. Not all. Sara's position was still not clear to me.

"What's the matter, Rona?" called Helen maliciously. She had found a plastic float and she was paddling the length of the pool. "Afraid to get your expensive bathing suit wet?"

"She's got a headache," called Cookie happily. "Have a nice headache, Rona!"

"This is the deep end," called Marlene, as she paddled. "Come on in!"

"Heather is going to be born swimming," pronounced Baby proudly. "When she swims in the mountain pool all the little fishes are going to nibble at her toes and blow bubbles at her, aren't they, Sara?"

I didn't even see Rona get up. I was watching Sara roll and slide in the water. Rona must have pulled off her slacks and shirt. Suddenly she was at poolside. And then she was in.

"Rona!" I called to her. "Are you allowed to swim?"

"Screw you!" she called as she began to swim the pool in long experienced strokes. I crouched awkwardly at the edge. "Rona, come on out!"

Rona reached the limits of the pool, turned, looked angrily at the spectators who were laughing at her, pushed away from the wall and kicked off for another lap.

Nurse Caulfield came running to poolside, a bottle of aspirin in hand. "Rona! Get the hell out of there!"

"What's the matter!" taunted Helen. "Are we going to poison her?"

Nurse Caulfield was pulling at her slacks when Rona surfaced, floated for a moment moaning "Help," and slid beneath the water.

"Hail Mary," said Mary Lou. "I didn't mean it!"

In that split second before the action started I had a vision. I had always suspected that when the crisis came, truly came upon me, that my petrifying fear of the water would dissipate. I felt that in the crisis I would throw myself into the water and swim. I knew it. I was sure of it.

Nurse Caulfield was over the side.

"Help her!" called Sara.

Marlene dived for her.

I leaped to the side of the pool, tried to throw myself in, clothes and all. I froze absolutely at the edge. Unable. Failed. Rigid, while the action progressed around me.

The hostesses ran with a life preserver. Rona was on the surface now, lifted by Sara and Nurse Caulfield. Rona only coughing, not dead. Even Mary Lou helped her, the elegant hair in wet snakes on her face. And I, on my knees, ingloriously helping to drag the inert body over the side, kneeling in a puddle of water.

"Can't move," moaned Rona. "Going to die . . ."

"Get some towels," Nurse Caulfield ordered. "Rona, you dummy. I told you not to swim."

And so I, chaperone of the Senior Class of Huntington House, ran for towels. Over my shoulder I saw the girls, Rona's enemies, surrounding her, patting her, comforting her. I returned with towels supplied by ladies who were terribly controlled and cool in contrast to my general anxiety. Rona's head was in Sara's lap.

"Somebody loaned me a bigger car," said Nurse Caulfield as

she pulled her clothes over her wet suit. "I'll take her to the hospital. She'll be okay."

"What's wrong with her? She scarcely ate a thing. Was it cramps?"

"I'm the dummy," she said. "I only wanted her to come because she was depressed. She's got sickle cell. She went into sickle cell shock. I should have had more sense."

Between us we carried Rona's heavy body to a chauffeured Rolls. The girls walked beside us, adding a hand to support the inert form.

"Can you drive the rest of them home?" asked Nurse Caulfield.

"We can!" said a contrite Cookie. "I'll leave my suitcase. They can ride in the back."

"Let me die," moaned Rona. "Let my baby die."

"Not on your life," said Nurse Caulfield. "Look at the car you're going to ride in, Rony."

Rona turned her limp head. "It's not so much," she said.

Rona was stretched out in the back seat, her head in Nurse Caulfield's lap, a Pasadena lady sitting guardian over her with a bottle of smelling salts. The car lurched forward, and they were gone.

"Please," begged one of the ladies, "we've not yet cut the cake."

And so the Senior Class and the Senior Class sponsor returned to poolside. We warmed ourselves in the sun, silently concerned, eating pieces of white cake with the announcement in fluffy frosting, Congratulations, Seniors.

I was still damp from the poolside fiasco. And chagrined. Sara lifted herself on one elbow, looked at me. "When Heather has her first birthday I'm not going to have one of these cakes with refined sugars. We'll bake our cake out of natural grains and we'll put sweet fruits and honey on the top. And we'll give her puffballs for gifts and she'll blow them and tickle her nose."

"Oh, Heather!" laughed Baby, clapping her hands. "I love her so much."

Gail brought her cake and sat beside us, shivering although the sun was high and hot against the tiles.

Sara watched me. She seemed in general content, at peace. I was not.

"What surprised me about you, Sara," I said frankly, "is how decent you were to Rona after she tried to hurt you."

"I understand her," said Sara sagely. "People act that way when they don't know how to love. We're all sisters, only when we're unhappy we act lousy. If you understand it's okay."

I thought seriously about her statement. It was too simple. Simplistic. But I had to know. I ventured a bold question. "Do you love your people in Omaha?"

She turned on her side, covered her face with her arm. "Rona and I were sisters. She told us her sadness when she thought she was going to die."

"People talk," said Gail, "when they think death is on them. It's a terrible feeling to die."

My bold question remained unanswered. Or perhaps the silence answered it.

"Do you mean *feeling*?" I said to Gail. "Death probably has no *feeling*."

"Don't you know your *Caesar*?" she asked me. "Cowards die many times before their deaths."

"I suppose so," I said, "in a manner of speaking."

"This is just a manner of dying. It's like Sartre. There's no exit. We didn't know that she was trapped in the same room with us."

"How didn't you know? She was pregnant, wasn't she?"

"You're dense," said Sara. "Like pea soup. Is that what you think the trouble is? Pregnant? That's the best part of it. Rona's got a black man's sickness and a white man's baby. Where do you go if you're stuck in a box like that?"

She looked at my face for response. I had none. I was still damp. And anxious about Rona. And confused about her. And humiliated from my ultimate lack of heroism.

"If you come and visit me," said Sara, "while my brothers and sisters are playing in the fields with Heather, I'll teach you how to swim."

Et Tu, Hester Prynne?

"WHAT DO YOU MEAN you're going to teach *The Scarlet Letter* to a bunch of pregnant girls! That's pretty heartless if you ask me."

But J. was less caustic than usual. In fact, since my swimming-party disaster he had been, I thought, rather gentle.

"Why is it heartless?" I asked between sips. "Hester Prynne was pregnant too. And miserable too."

"So why do you keep reminding them of their condition?"

"How can they ignore it? Almost every senior is due to deliver soon. They get bigger every day, right before my eyes. Their belly buttons are so pushed out they can't sit next to the tables anymore. And their backs hurt. And I want Sara to read this book because it bothers me to hear her go on with this terrible fantasy."

"Why is it a terrible fantasy? Why isn't it a wonderful fantasy?"

"Because she's going to be horribly disappointed when she has a funny-looking boy baby without hair and when the Prince Charming in the bus fails to show up to pay the doctor's bills. And you still have to sterilize bottles for little Heathers of the fields."

"Don't you think it's odd that you mentioned cold sterile bottles when she'll probably have the child suckling at her warm breast? And what *if* she might be disappointed? Does that mean she ought to be miserable the whole nine months in advance? For a logician your logic confounds me."

"Are you actually *saying* that people ought to delude themselves with false hope?"

"You wouldn't know what's false and what's real," he had the nerve to say. "Why is hope a delusion? And why are all your seniors due at the same time? Did they all conceive in the full of the moon? Or do you group them according to moment of conception?"

"It's the holiday theory. They get pregnant on Christmas or Easter or the Fourth of July or the night before school starts or on a three-day holiday in Lake Arrowhead. They get a terrible need to be loved. It's psychological. And they have to satisfy their need."

"Why their need?" he asked. "Why only *their* need?"

"Most people are more civilized, aren't they? Most people don't wear their ids so close to the surface. Most people don't lose control of their lives."

"Tonight is a holiday," breathed J. "It's the end of a holiday. Come with me down by the sea where the waves smack the rocks and the little sandpipers run away from the edge of the tide."

"What holiday?"

"The Cinco de Mayo, for God's sake. Come run with me by the water's wild edge."

I had never realized that he was so poetic.

"I can't. I have to make lesson plans for *The Scarlet Letter.*"

"Naturally," he said. I think he was really angry.

"Honestly, if I don't start right I'll ruin the whole unit."

"I never doubted your honesty. And I don't want to ruin your unit. That's the last thing in the world I would want to ruin. Enjoy yourself."

He hung up.

What he needed was a good cup of tea.

.

I was carrying a stack of *Scarlet Letters* when Doris caught me.

"The classics!" she exclaimed. "Splendid. There is nothing like the classics to uplift the spirit."

I did not feel kindly toward Doris.

"I'm instructing, Doris, not uplifting. There is nothing uplifting about a gullible Puritan girl who has sexual intercourse under the pines with a fast-talking minister."

I think she was dismayed. "Is that a new version?"

I headed toward the stairs to avoid any other early-morning literary critics. I passed Sara at the hall phone. Nothing unusual. Girls often received calls either before or after schooltime. But her hands stopped me. When I saw her hands I realized that she was talking to the boy in the VW bus.

One hand held the phone, clutched it to her ear. The other flew like a bird, fluttered in midair as she paused to listen, pressing the phone against her ear to hear, swooping through the air as she heard his voice once more, caressing the mouthpiece of the phone as if it were the object and not merely the means. Her voice was music. And a bare foot that had kicked off her sandal dug into the linoleum.

He had actually called.

But the music stopped. The bird became a hand, flopped dead at her side. She held the phone to her ear, her toe flattened against the cold ground. I think she shivered. She replaced the phone without a farewell.

I was ashamed to be standing when she turned. She was angry. Not because I was eavesdropping. No.

It was my expression that infuriated her. "I didn't *ask* him for Heather, did I! He didn't even know, did he! I just wanted her myself because . . ." She choked in recollection and in pain. I tried to withdraw myself. I was devastated that the boy, the father of heavenly Heather, wasn't coming back. Not that I ever expected him. But to call her and to give her those moments of hope. And then to disappoint her. It was hideous.

"You don't have to *look* that way! Just because he's not coming this minute doesn't mean he's not coming. He has to work out this hang-up!"

Foolish Sara. "Does he have a hang-up?"

"Don't you? Doesn't everyone?"

It wasn't right that she should continue this delusion. It wasn't right that she should hang on to something that had just been irrevocably snatched from her. It was too dangerous.

"No, I don't have any hang-up. Most people, most logical people, function quite well."

She waved her wild hair, stamped her foot. "But functioning isn't living, is it!"

She turned and stalked off to the dining room. And I climbed the steps. Stupid of her. Not to see the truth and deal with the truth. So absorbed in my own anger that I bumped into Cookie. But when I looked up to apologize it wasn't Cookie at all. Mary Lou in Cookie's sequined eyelashes and Cookie's hair. She squeezed past me.

"My boyfriend came," she muttered.

I turned in amazement and followed her as she descended toward the visitors' room. Cookie came lumbering down the stairs. "What happened to Mary Lou?" I asked her.

"*Poor* Mary Lou. I'm so sorry for her. He came and her hair wasn't even up. So I loaned her my wig." Cookie wore a head of hair that was entirely unfamiliar.

We descended together and peered carefully from the edge of the doorway to see the boyfriend.

It was indeed a soldier. And he and Mary Lou sat, not beside but across from each other. Stiff and uncomfortable.

A soldier. At least he wore the uniform of the United States Army. Neither Athens nor Sparta would have claimed him with much pride. He was fat. His neck pressed against the collar of his uniform and the buttons of his shirt bulged against his protruding stomach.

Cookie and I both turned and started upstairs. "Boy," she said. And that was about it.

I sat second period with a stack of mimeographed guides to *The Scarlet Letter* before me, and a cluster of bewildered girls, each bent in her own direction. Sara's eyes opaque almost. I don't believe she saw anything beyond her own confusion. Trying to piece the dream and the world together. Mary Lou had her own hair down. She tugged at her crucifix, moved her lips in some inner argument or perhaps some prayer.

Gail was immersed in a book but from time to time she looked to Sara for signs of change. Helen was not writing but reading a letter.

"Tell about Heather," begged Baby. "Tell how funny it will be the first time she wears shoes. Tell how her first shoes will be made of some dead animal but an animal that died already so she won't wear anything that had to be killed and how you'll soften the leather by chewing on it. Tell it, Sara."

Sara opened her eyes in Baby's direction but did not see her. She merely shook her head, trying to clear it of what was confounding her.

But Mary Lou made whatever adjustment was necessary. "He only had a short leave but he'll be here longer when he gets a three-day pass."

Sara breathed out heavily. No. She blew, as if something pressing on her heart needed to come out, or as if there was a fog about her which needed a sharp wind to dissipate it, or as if the force of the blowing would calm her heart.

"I think we have time for one more novel before we have to start on graduation speeches," I began. "And so I want you to start *The Scarlet Letter*."

"If it's going to be more people falling off a bridge I'm not going to read it," stated Cookie.

"Tell more about Heather's first words," said Baby, looking anxiously toward Sara. "How she'll say 'I love you' in baby talk."

This was my final unit. And I would teach it. And I would not compete with a baby named Heather saying "I wuv you." How would our librarian capture their interest? Because this book was right. I knew it.

"This one is a love story about a beautiful Puritan girl who has trapped herself in marriage to an old crippled intellectual."

"Those marriages work out okay," said Cookie, "if the old guy has money."

"But he sends her off to the New World and for a few years he doesn't show up."

"Why not?" asked Marlene, who was supposed to be reading *Teen Tales*.

"He was captured by Indians."

"Indians!" snorted Sara. Up out of the fog. "Why do they always make Indians the villains? Do you know what disgusting things we did to their buffalo? We sliced steaks from living animals and left them howling in pain to die. And the Indians worshiped the earth and carried their little ones on their backs. And you say the Indian was the villain!"

"Sara, the plight of the Indian isn't the point. The point is that in this Puritan community poor lonely and forlorn Hester Prynne finds a new companion and suddenly she is with child."

"With whose child?" asked Helen, looking up from her letter.

"That's a euphemism," said Gail. "It means pregnant."

"Don't tell me that Puritans actually got pregnant," said Sara. "I thought they never got undressed."

It was good to hear the acrid tones. At least she was fighting back.

"Who said you had to get undressed to get pregnant?" asked Cookie.

"The minister had severe psychiatric problems," said Gail. "Hawthorne was ahead of his time in his concept of analysis."

"The minister!" screamed Cookie. "She got screwed by a minister? Young or old?"

"Young," said Gail. "He was a famous orator."

"Did they do *that* in those days?" exclaimed Cookie.

"Hey," said Helen to Mary Lou. "How come your boyfriend left so fast."

"He had to visit his mother."

"And I want to start the symbolism in the first chapter so please discuss your F.O.B.'s after class. The most interesting fact is that each symbol in this symbolic novel has a double meaning and a meaning that is significant to our own lives."

"Is that why he came?" asked Helen. "To tell you he had to go?"

"He came to get his mother's ring. She has to have it back to wear to this big family party, so they won't think it's lost. It's an heirloom."

"Don't!" shrieked Cookie. "Don't give anything back until you talk to me!"

"He'll bring it on his next leave," said Mary Lou.

"Don't be a jerk," said Cookie. "Never give back anything. Once you get it it belongs to you."

"Leave her alone," said Sara. "She trusts him. You have to trust people you love."

"Some trust," muttered Cookie. "Like the girl trusted the minister. Did he tell about being her F.O.B.?"

"She had to stand on the scaffold with the baby in her arms," said Gail, "so that the people could ridicule her."

"Establishment!" accused Sara.

"Gail, don't give the plot away."

"The plot isn't important," said Gail. "On the edge of the crowd was a crippled but very intelligent man."

"I know who it was," said Cookie. "He was an older man who was willing to marry her and take the baby in exchange for her young body. I read it in *Modern Romances*."

"It was her husband," said Gail. "Her old intellectual husband."

"Gail, please don't spoil the story."

"How can you spoil it?" said Sara. "It's spoiled already. Indians!" she said in mock exasperation.

"My thesis," said Gail, "is that Hester Prynne actually represents the Church of England and Hester has actually seduced the minister in order to purify the church. It's a religious allegory."

"What happened to the baby?" asked Sara. "Did the establishment try to take her baby?"

"They tried," said Gail, "but she wouldn't let them."

"Good for her!" said Sara. "The young minister will come for her and take her to live with the Indians if she has faith and waits for him."

"He'll save the baby," laughed Baby. "And they'll live with the Indians like Heather will."

Sara whipped around and looked at Baby with such a plea, such pain that Baby was subdued.

"That's not the way the story is written," I said.

"What kind of a letter is it?" asked Helen. "Who wrote it?"

"The Scarlet Letter is an A," I explained. "It stands for adultery. Hester has to wear it forever on her breast."

"Like a tattoo?" asked Helen.

"On the top of her clothing."

"That's an easy sentence. She could of just took it off."

"That's the point. Let's start the first chapter. Because the book was written about a period in history when adultery was a sin that burned deep in the hearts of all the characters. And that's where we get our symbolism."

"What sin?" asked Sara. "Love isn't a sin. It's a religious act. Love is the only religious act in the world."

"Not in my church," said Mary Lou.

"You and your church," said Sara. "If it's such a sin why did you do it?"

Mary Lou slumped in her chair. "Satan tempted me."

"He sure tempted you with a fat soldier," said Cookie.

"You'll notice on the guide sheet that the first symbol is the baby Pearl."

"What does she do when they try to take her baby away?" demanded Sara.

"She threatens the man she loves," said Gail. "She'll disclose his name if he doesn't defend their child."

"I know I read it in *Modern Romances*," said Cookie.

"It's a cruel thing to make her choose between her love and the child," said Sara. "That's what your generation does," she said to me. " 'Choose!' " she mimicked, in whose voice I didn't know. " 'Make up your mind,' " she mimicked again. And then in her own voice, "As if you can't have the whole thing! As if when you're happy with the whole thing they get frightened and try to take a part of it away."

"There are a number of possible themes I want you to note. Flowers, the dark, the light . . ."

"She needed the minister," said Sara. "She wanted him because he could give her something the old husband and his generation couldn't. And if she couldn't have the minister then at least she'd have the baby. At least she'd have Heather and no-body could take her away."

"Pearl," said Gail. "The baby's name is Pearl."

"I *said* Pearl," answered Sara angrily.

Nobody disputed her.

"And the scaffold is the pivotal chapter. It appears three times. Three is a magic number in *The Scarlet Letter*."

"She should have married the Indian," said Cookie. "Indians are very loyal."

"Or the novel could have been a political satire," said Gail. "Old Prynne could be degenerate Europe and Hester, the rape of the Virgin New World by the missionaries."

"So Chapter One finds Hester just coming out of the prison with her newborn baby, and when we read it you'll see the tor-ment she feels when she faces the mob."

"Is he the kind of minister who can get married?" asked Cookie.

"She's married already," said Gail. "Remember the old hus-band."

"But her old husband could kick off and leave her the insur-ance and she could go to church for the funeral and this minister is preaching the sermon and he sees her so beautiful standing by the coffin."

"Does it have a happy ending?" asked Marlene. "Can we read it too?"

"Yes, it has a happy ending," said Sara. "It *has*. When the old husband sees how Hester loves the minister he divorces her and the minister takes her and her baby to live in the forest. And they call the baby Pearl because she is the jewel of their lives. She shines so bright that she lights their path when they walk in the dark night."

"They called her Pearl," said Gail, "because she was a pearl of great price."

"You should never have given back the ring," said Cookie to Mary Lou.

"If my boyfriend gets a three-day pass he's going to convert Catholic," said Mary Lou. "He promised when I gave him the ring. I believe him because it's a holy promise. If he doesn't do it God will punish him."

"He already looks pretty punished to me," said Cookie.

"So are we ready to start *The Scarlet Letter?*"

"Start it?" asked Cookie. "I thought we finished it!"

Mother's Day

FINALLY!" I told J. "At last I found a novel they can relate to. I admit they digress. But they always digress. I'm beginning to understand the way pregnancy shortens the attention span."

"I'm very interested in pregnant attention spans," said J. "I only hope that your bit of satisfaction is worth it. I only hope that you understand the relative value of things. I only hope your goddamned compositions are worth the most beautiful night of the year. I hope that every crummy punctuation mark is worth more than the moon on the goddamned rocks!"

"And they empathize with Hester. They really do. You should have heard Sara, the way she saw herself in the book. She *was* Hester. She *was* standing on the pillory with the minister's baby in her arms, bravely rejecting the scorn of the community. And how do you know that the moon was so beautiful if you didn't go?"

"Who said I didn't go?"

". . . I see."

"I doubt it, by the tone of your voice."

"There is no tone to my voice. I'm glad you went. I really am. That's what I've always said about our independence. I don't see why you shouldn't have gone just because my work obliges me to stay home."

"All right. I agree."

"Only if I'm not intruding on your privacy, whom did you go with?"

I wasn't making a thing of it. I was just curious.

"If I *had* gone with anyone," he sputtered, "if I *had* gone, I wouldn't have gone with a *whom!*"

J. is so predictable.

"So now that they're involved with Hester Prynne I'm going to teach the metaphor the way the metaphor ought to be taught. The snake of a tremor across the face. And the matron with snow in her bosom."

"You're very clever," said J. "If I were in your class I would absolutely be able to visualize the snake of a tremor."

"Well, thank you." I didn't often have compliments from J. At least not about my work.

"But aside from these earth-shaking metaphors what is it you want them to learn? That they made the same mistake as Hester? That they didn't take the pill and they have to wear scarlet letters for the rest of their lives? Exactly what did you have in mind to teach them?"

"You don't understand," I explained to him. "I don't teach what *I* believe. I teach subject matter. They have to reach their own conclusions."

"But what are *your* conclusions? How do you feel about them? Do you think they're only stupid kids? Do you empathize with them? Do you *like* them?

"How I feel isn't the point. I don't make judgments."

"The hell you don't! The judgments you make with your tone of voice are louder than any of your fancy metaphors. If the girls are beginning to feel like Hester, you'd better make sure of what's in Pandora's box."

I did not hang up. I simply said goodbye.

I was sure that what he said was not true. He was unkind because he was piqued. I was understanding enough not to take him seriously.

.

I climbed the steps the next morning absorbed in the metaphor. A stern community of rigid pines. The stream of life rushing along. And the pearl of great price.

And Pandora's box.

So absorbed that I collided with one of the girls in the entry. "Watch where you're going," she snapped. But I knew her. And she was not a girl and she was not a resident of Huntington House. She was pregnant, not young, fatigued, squat, muscular, her face set in harsh lines. And the resemblance to her daughter was uncanny. This was Ada.

I paused at the secretary's desk and looked back to the entry. It had to be Ada. This was Helen's mother.

Suddenly Doris was standing beside me, one hand clutching a copy of *The Scarlet Letter*, the other pointing in accusation. "There is nothing pornographic in this book. I read this entire book and there is no hint of pornography."

"Who said there was?"

"You! You implied!"

"Doris, you inferred."

"I did not infer anything that wasn't implicitly implied."

"Honi soit qui mal y pense," I said. "Evil is she who evil thinketh."

I could not swim but I indulged in other sports.

Doris flushed with inturned anger.

Let her flush.

"I may visit your class today," she articulated, syllable by syllable, holding her tongue carefully to prevent it from saying anything accidental.

"Excellent," I articulated back to her. "I'll expect you. I'm teaching the metaphor."

"I hope you are teaching like and as," she enunciated.

"Like and as what?"

"If it has *like* in front of it, it is a simile and if it doesn't it is a metaphor."

"*Like* is irrelevant, Doris. The metaphor is a poetic concept, not a structural device."

The pregnant visitor squeezed between us, edged up to the desk. "Where's the kid? I been waiting half an hour."

The old secretary looked almost disappointed that my discussion with Doris had been interrupted.

Helen stamped into the office. It *was* Ada, pregnant in her middle age. In contrast to the freshness of the mothers of Huntington House, her pregnancy seemed to emphasize the aging process which was unkind. Mother and daughter confronted without formalities, both tough, both angry. They stood belly to belly.

"Listen," demanded Ada. "Did you get a letter?"

Helen smiled a Cheshire smile. "Who from?"

The smile, closer to a smirk, struck a familiar spark, flared. "You know damn well who from! Don't give me none of your lies." There was exhaustion in the lines of her face, in the slump of her body. "I told you and told you he was a rat. I ain't got no money. I'm on the County."

"Big deal. You was on the County before you met him."

"I'm gonna take the law to him."

"For what? He ain't done anything to you. He could say he hit you because you was running around."

"I wasn't and you know it," screamed Ada.

"I don't know nothing! You was rotten to him and he run off. You should of been nice." She leered at her mother. "He was always nice to me."

Ada looked at her daughter's belly and then touched her own. "You little bitch!" she managed to say before the tears came. She turned and stalked out, slamming the door behind her.

Miss Rodriguiz popped into the office. "Do you want a loud-speaker?" she asked Helen. "Why don't you broadcast to the whole house?"

Helen simply laughed. She winked at me, drew an envelope from the pocket of her blouse, waved it at me. She was still laughing as she climbed the stairs.

The two pregnant women. And the letter. Helen and her midnight trysts with the lascivious stepfather. And the pregnant wife lying sleepless in bed, waiting for her husband to come. It was Faulknerian.

"Great pair," said Miss Rodriguiz.

"Shameless," said the old secretary.

"Dishonorable," said Doris.

"Poor Helen," I said to Miss Rodriguiz as she led me away from the secretary's desk, out of earshot.

"She's not the only one you can hear all over the house. Why do you bait Doris that way?"

"Bait her? I? She's picked on me since the day I came."

"Didn't you ever take any psych? There is no suggestion she's made to you that isn't absolutely sincere. From the bottom of her heart. She can't help her limitations. Now you can just swallow it and have a laugh or you can be defensive. And when you're defensive she's aggressive. And when she's not you are. It's childish."

She walked out, making notes on her clipboard. Leaving me standing there.

"By the way," called the secretary, "there's someone in the visitors' room."

Social workers! They take a couple of units in counseling and they think they're Jung. She didn't know of half the encounters. The provocative overtones. And undertones. And the business about the swimming!

I came out of my anger to see someone's mother and father sitting uncomfortably on the plastic sofa. A sad genial couple, crowded together, timorous and apologetic. I was getting used to them. I had already seen dozens on the day they brought their daughters to Huntington House. Sitting nervously on the edge of their seats, clutching hands. The man graying, rather attractive. The woman tailored, a generous smile edged in discomfort. I liked them. And I was sorry for them. Did J. think I didn't sympathize with their anguish? I hoped their daughter was a senior because by the shape of things I might be losing a few before graduation.

The man rose, extended his hand to me.

"I'm glad we caught you before we left. We wanted to find out if she's making progress. She's a fine student you know. At least she was before all this."

Her mother smiled wistfully. "She won a medal in the science fair. Did she tell you? She made her own machine to detect radiation. All by herself. We have the award in a glass case at home."

"Nothing in her room has been touched," said the father. "So that she can bridge the gap when she comes home. I've always had the feeling that she'll be a fine scholar one of these days."

"I have every paper she ever wrote," said the mother, as I tried to register what scientifically inclined girl was in any of my classes.

"I'm sorry . . ."

"Ah," said the father, "I thought the secretary told you. We're Sara's parents."

Omaha, Nebraska! This man holding his wife's hand, smiling

to her at my confusion. Could this be the ogre who scattered money on open wounds?

"I suppose she's said awful things about us," said the mother, gently. "But you know this rebellious period. They test their wings. They have to shake the nest before they can leave it. But a little time and experience leads them back to truth. Don't you think?"

"She's a bright girl," was the most ambiguous answer I could give.

"I'm sorry this happened to her," said her father, "but things have a way of turning around. I know that girl better than she knows herself."

"We'll just stay on until graduation or until she has the baby. I don't think the boy will come back, do you?"

I listened to the tone of her question. It seemed innocent, without recrimination. Just a question.

"She claims she doesn't want to graduate," said the father, "but she will. When the chips are down they always do. As sophisticated as they pretend to be, the ceremony means something to them. The way we turned from the church when her mother and I were young and came back when we got our senses. I'm glad you're giving her *The Scarlet Letter*. I always enjoy teaching that book."

"Do you teach?" I asked him.

"Of course we teach," said Sara's mother. "Didn't she tell you?"

•

I wanted to see her. To watch her face and to see how she would react. The parents confused me. They seemed concerned. Seemed. And Sara in her anger genuine. All seemed.

Her chair was empty.

"Where's Sara?"

"Not feeling well," said Gail.

"Is she having false labor?" asked Baby apprehensively. "Is Heather coming?"

"There are many labors," said Gail, looking herself a bit apprehensive. "Sara is gathering her strength to meet the foe."

But who was Sara's foe? The kindly couple downstairs?

It was time for the metaphor and my class had lost its momentum. I could smell nail polish. Cookie's head bent over her task. And Helen was absorbed in her letter. Mary Lou had her uncoifed head down on her desk. Gail had taken up a book. Edna St. Vincent Millay. Only Marlene and Baby, who should have been reading *Teen Tales*, gave me their undivided attention.

"By definition," I began, "the metaphor is a comparison between things that aren't really alike but have like qualities. But it isn't the definition that is important. It is the *feeling* of a metaphor and the depth of understanding that comes with it."

"What's she talking about?" asked Helen, not even bothering to look up from her letter.

"Love is not all," said Gail, closing the book and reciting from memory, "it is not meat nor drink nor slumber nor a roof against the rain; nor yet a floating spar to men who sink and rise and sink and rise again."

"Exactly. Gail has marvelous recall. The line is full of beautiful metaphors."

"What's beautiful about a person drowning?" asked Cookie.

"It doesn't mean that a person is actually drowning. It just compares love with a drowning person to tell what love is."

"Why does it say a person is drowning if he isn't? I don't see how it makes you understand a book more. It makes you understand it less."

"Not if you understand metaphors. In the book one line tells us that a matron of the town who was unkind to Hester carried *snow* in her bosom."

"So?" asked Cookie, looking up from her painted nails. She

saw me staring at her artwork and she held them up for me to see. "False. Because my real ones broke. I have to polish them because the joints show. I can't have stumpy fingers."

"There!" I said. "That's a metaphor. Stumps of fingers is a metaphor. Your fingers can't actually be stumps."

"Sure they're stumps. That's what they look like with broken nails."

"A stump is a remainder of a tree after it's been cut down. Your finger isn't a remainder of a tree but it looks like a remainder of a tree. So it's a metaphor." I couldn't have asked for a more pertinent example. "Like the snow in the matron's bosom. She couldn't actually have carried snow in her bosom."

"Why not?" asked Cookie. "Did you ever go on a winter holiday in Lake Arrowhead? We used to fall down and stuff snow in all kinds of places. It was fun."

"Cookie, you missed the point. There wasn't actually any *snow*. It simply meant that the feeling she had in her heart was coldness. She had a cold heart."

"Cold heart is also a metaphor," Gail corrected me. "No heart is cold unless an evil spirit catches it in a center of wickedness and chills it. Some mothers have cold hearts."

"Are there evil spirits?" asked Baby, alarmed.

Whose mothers? Did she mean her mother or Sara's mother who seemed to have a warm heart. Seemed.

"Excellent. Very perceptive. Of course a heart can't actually be cold."

"Unless you're dead," said Gail, "which some of us are."

"Cross yourself," warned Mary Lou. "Cut it out."

"Look at it this way. You make a comparison between things that have similar qualities but are actually different."

"Teachers always say things that don't make sense," said Mary Lou. "The Sisters teach clearer."

"Look," I explained. "Take clouds for instance. The clouds are like what?"

There was no answer.

"Come on. If you look at the sky the clouds remind you of something. What do they remind you of?"

"They remind you that if you don't take an umbrella," said Cookie, fashioning a neat turn of the brush, "that it will probably rain cats and dogs."

"That's it! Exactly! It doesn't actually rain cats and dogs!"

"Sure it does. In the winter it rains cats and dogs."

"Not *actually* cats and dogs. Cats and dogs don't come falling out of the sky. Dachshunds and Dalmatians and Siamese cats and Pekingeses don't rain out of the clouds."

"She's crazy," said Helen.

"How about Cockapoos?" laughed Baby.

"For instance take the name Cookie. Somebody compared Cookie with a sweet thing. A cookie is sweet. So that Cookie's mother must have thought her very sweet when she was a baby."

"My mother calls me *Laverne*," she said pointedly.

"Then who calls you Cookie?"

"Don't ask," she said.

It was then I became aware of Doris standing in the doorway. She did not speak. She walked directly to the blackboard. She picked up a piece of chalk and in her even, impeccable script she wrote:

Her eyes were *like* stars.	Simile.
Her eyes were stars.	Metaphor.

"If it has the word *like* or *as*," she stated, "it is a simile. And if it does *not* have the word *like* or *as*, it is a metaphor." She brushed the chalk dust from her fingers and walked deliberately from the room.

"That's easier," said Mary Lou, copying the phrases. "That's more like the Sisters."

"Recognizing the metaphor isn't understanding it," I answered bleakly. "Do you understand what a metaphor *is*?"

"Sure," said Mary Lou. "It's a word without *like* or *as*." She seemed absolutely satisfied.

"Just read," I suggested. The balloon of my spirits was punctured. I was deflated. I was an empty vessel. I was a teacher in a sea of confusion without a spar. I was finished for the hour.

They opened their books, I'm sure *not* to read. Perhaps to dream. Let them.

Helen plunked down in a chair beside me. Carefully she unfolded her letter and placed it before me.

> Hi kid. Long time no see. Ada sure is sore. I miss your cooking. Remember keep your mouth shut. Be a good kid. Don't start nothing with Ada. She can make real trouble. After you have "it" I'll see can I fix it so you can stay with me. I'll write "if." Don't tell Ada I wrote you.
>
> Mike

I read her letter with a face that did not, I hope, show editorial comment. Because I was disgusted by the fantasy it created — the man Mike, grizzled and derelict, in a rumpled unmade bed with both women, seducing first the mother and then the daughter, the matching bellies, the lascivious leer.

Helen's fingers lovingly touched the edge of the grimy notepaper on which the words were scrawled. I noticed for the first time that one of her fingers was tattooed. An L and a dot. She noticed my gaze and held the finger for me to see.

"Every guy in the gang tattooed his property. I ain't his property no more. I ain't even gonna let him see the baby."

"Let who see what?"

"Let my F.O.B. see the baby."

She smiled grandly at my error. "You thought it was Mike's!" She laughed, slapping her thigh in delight. "So does Ada!"

I had never seen her so pleased with herself. "I don't understand. Why should you want her to think something that just isn't true?"

She sobered quickly, folded her letter carefully, placed it tenderly in her blouse pocket. "She yelled at them and chased them off. Now let *her* see what it's like to be by herself. Because *I* got the letter. For *one* time I wanted a thing and I got it. And she can think whatever she goddamn pleases."

A Pearl of Great Price

EVERYBODY had a copy of my mimeographed assignment but Sara. And she was the one who had inspired it. So I felt impelled to give her a copy. I hadn't sent it with Gail because, I suppose, there was something I needed to know for myself. Was Sara the thankless child who spurned the love of her parents for some redwoods bum? Or a child neglected and deprived of the solace of the heart.

I had never visited the rooms before because I felt that the girls were entitled to their privacy. All of the corridors seemed to be basically alike but through half-opened doors I could see stuffed animals and bright chenille spreads and posters.

I knew their room immediately. Over Mary Lou's bed hung a plastic Jesus looking mournfully down at her pillow. Beside the bed on the old table was an American flag, an unopened Bible, and a bag of hair curlers. Across the room was Gail's bed, unmade and loaded with books. Books on the chair and books on the floor. The walls were unadorned. Sara's bed must have been behind the door. And so I knocked.

I heard movement from the third bed. "Go away," she said.

"Hi!" I called through the door that separated us. "I have an assignment for you. Are you feeling all right?" I paused for reply.

"Oh it's you," she said without much enthusiasm. "Come in if you want to."

The bed was hers and the corner was hers. Driftwood and bits of cloth and stones, a macramé hanging. A poster which proclaimed POT! A picture of a mountain. And at her bedside fresh flowers. Where she had found flowers I didn't know. Perhaps she had been scavenging in the neighborhood gardens. Sara herself lay uncovered, the hill of her stomach pressing her into the bed. Her arms and legs sprawled listlessly. She stared at the ceiling.

"You met them."

"Your parents? Yes. They introduced themselves before I came up this morning."

"They charmed you, naturally. A bunch of teachers all together talking teacher-talk."

"I didn't even know they were teachers until your mother told me. You never mentioned."

"Come on. You gravitated together like magnets. You're all the same species."

I had no answer. Yes, I liked them.

"I suppose they showed you my science medal. They carry it around in a glass showcase and display it whenever they get a crowd of one."

"They didn't show me your science medal."

"I'll bet."

"They mentioned it."

"Naturally. Well what's the message? What did they send you up to say? You know it's not your age that holds you together. It's the same glue."

"I didn't come as a messenger."

"Then I suppose you came to bring me a topic sentence. Do you want me to write a paragraph on the most unforgettable parents I ever knew, or what?"

"I had some notes on the metaphor."

"Naturally."

I rose to go. I was hurt that I had been misinterpreted. But I did have the notes in my hand after all. What *could* she have thought?

"To tell the truth I came up to see how you were feeling. I missed you second period and the girls said you didn't feel well and I was worried."

I laid the notes on her table near a small sea-washed pebble and I turned to leave.

"Okay," she said. "Stay if you want."

But I was feeling uncomfortable and out of place. "I'll see you in class tomorrow."

"Stay," she said. "I want you to. Please."

And so I sat by her bed. She kept her eyes on the ceiling, tracing the hairline cracks in the air with her fingers as she spoke.

"What did you think of them?" Her question seemed general enough and without anger. But I weighed my answer carefully.

"They were concerned about you."

"They are all right. They are concerned."

She focused her eyes on the cracks, trying to read something into the random lines.

"Do you remember," she asked, "in the book where they call Pearl the pearl of great price?"

"It's a metaphor."

"I *know* it's a metaphor. I had science prizes and I was a genius before I fell from grace. Remember?"

She had been right on that first day. I did not know Sara at all. Because at the foot of her bed, protruding from rumpled bedclothes, I saw a paperback. *The Sun Also Rises* by Ernest Hemingway.

"Everything has a price. With them anyhow. You don't know

why I'm so mad at them, do you. I mean they're so gentlemanly and so cultured. Aren't they?"

There was no sarcasm in her voice.

"No, but I can guess."

"What do you guess?"

I hoped that it was a rhetorical question. I did not want to intrude on her private grief. There was nothing I could do to alleviate her pain.

She turned on her side to face me. "I want you to answer. Otherwise I wouldn't have asked you. I don't play your kind of games. I just ask straight out and all you have to do is answer straight out."

"Then I guess that they want you to give up Heather. And I know how much it means to you to keep her."

"You're a lousy guesser," she said. "They came to tell me that they love me and they know I love my baby and they want me to come home. They'll give her a room of her own and they'll straighten her teeth when they come in crooked. The best of everything."

I listened in the silence to hear if she was weeping. She wasn't. But I could hear that her breathing was deep and anguished. She fell back on the bed, looking off into some place I could not follow.

"But that's good, isn't it? In a way it solves your problem."

"He's coming back," she said fiercely.

"Then you have two choices. That's more than most people have."

"But if he comes back he can't give her the best of everything, can he? I mean pediatricians and vitamins and nursery schools. He hasn't got a regular job. And he's not likely to get one. So he can't pay the tutors when she needs to learn the multiplication tables."

"But if it's the truth they were right to tell you, weren't they? You said that's what you wanted."

She pulled herself up, sat on the edge of the bed, facing me. "I could have got rid of her. You know. At the beginning when she was nothing. But I thought . . ." She fell back again. "It all got out of hand."

She was worn out. "I'll die back there. I'll go back to my old room with the science medals and I'll watch them eating grapefruit. They cut grapefruit into little even sections one at a time and read the editorials and watch the late news on TV. I'll die. What would you do if you were me?"

I wasn't going to answer for her life. "That's not a fair question. I can't make your decisions."

"I didn't *ask* you to make my decisions. I'm not going to run out and do what anyone tells me. Especially an English teacher. Especially not you. I just asked you. What would you do?" She reached out and took my hand and held it. She trapped me. If she wanted a straight answer, then I'd give it to her. I only hoped that she was prepared for it.

"If I were in your situation I'd probably give up the baby for adoption to someone who was prepared to love it and care for it and raise it the way I wanted it raised and pay for pediatricians, and then I'd go off somewhere and make my own life and study something and be independent so that I wouldn't have to make choices from any tight corners."

That's what I felt and that's what I told her. But the risk of saying it quite caught my breath. I felt my heart quicken. And I wished my words unsaid. I prepared for the caustic answer.

I didn't get one. She just took my hand and put it on the mountain of her stomach. I tried to pull it back but she held it tight. Then the flat of my hand felt movement, a great turning, a hump that rolled in her womb, rolled like Sara that day in the pool, a dolphin of a baby swimming under my hand. She held it there and asked me something with her eyes. Now there were tears on the edges of her lashes. Raindrops on the needles of her redwoods.

She released my hand. I had no other thing to say and so I left. At least someone had learned the meaning of the metaphor *pearl of great price.*

I had.

Shana and the Wrath of God

I CAN'T TELL YOU how moved I was when I felt Sara's baby," I told J. "As if suddenly I understood the intensity of their turmoil. And I wondered how I could possibly teach them without knowing the experience they were going through. How would *I* feel about studying with that going on inside of me. My whole planning has been wrong. There was a missing factor."

"If you want one it can be arranged," said J.

"One what?"

"One baby."

"Don't be stupid," I said. "Why is it when I talk about my teaching you always bring things to a personal level."

"Don't you ever call me stupid!" he said viciously. "Even as a joke. You . . . snow queen!"

"I didn't mean stupid denotatively. I only meant it in a manner of speaking. Why are you so sensitive? And why do you always make innuendoes? If you have something to say, say it right out."

"Right out? *What* innuendoes! You need an ear trumpet! How on earth do I get through to a vestal virgin!"

"Virgin! If *anyone* knows I'm not a virgin, *you* ought to know I'm not a virgin!"

"Your movable parts all function well. It's your *heart* that's virginal. You never give your true heart away. Never in your life! You are a virgin of the heart! You have snow in your bosom!"

"It's rotten to use my metaphors against me! And why are you being so hostile? I'm trying to tell you that Sara is teaching me something about teaching. And how can you imply that I have a heart of ice when I'm so full of emotion? Haven't you heard me read 'Patterns' by Amy Lowell? My God, when I get to the part about 'a pattern called a war. Christ! What are patterns for?' I cry all over the page. I don't even *teach* it anymore because I cry so much over the last lines."

"Exactly," said J. "If life were only written in iambic pentameter, kid, you'd have it made."

I didn't answer him. He had wounded me. I must have been very tired to let him get at me that way. In fact I hadn't been sleeping well.

"What's the matter?" he asked. "I don't hear any protest. Are you still there?"

"I want to go to the ocean. Right now."

"Oh you do. Right now."

"Yes, right now," I said.

"And why suddenly right now?"

"I'm very tense. You want me to be impetuous, don't you? You always make such a big thing about my being spontaneous. So I'm being spontaneous. I'm ready to go to the ocean."

"Are you?" he said.

"Yes," I said.

"With me in particular or with anyone who can untense you?"

The male mentality is so difficult to understand that I wonder that anyone *manages* to get pregnant.

"Come on," he said, now that he knew he had the advantage, "with *whom* did you want to go?"

I hung up.

Let him go soak his head in high tide.

You cannot reason with that man.

Rather, I should say, "one" cannot reason. Just because he up-set me was no cause for me to get sloppy.

.

I was in a lousy mood the next morning. I ran into Sara's parents coming down the steps as I came up. They smiled affa-bly, shaking my hand, patting my arm.

"She's coming around," he said. "Patience."

"And confidence," said the mother. I tried to get a clear look at her face, to see something that Sara saw, something villainous or something foreboding. What was there in the woman's face that made Sara run? She was a handsome woman. She looked like Sara.

I absolutely required a cup of tea before beginning my day. And so I took my cup into the tiny office of Miss Rodriguiz who absolutely required a cup of coffee before beginning hers.

"Most welcome," she said. "It's about time."

I sat in the cracked leather chair where the girls in their sor-row sat, where they took their gripes and problems. A couple of chairs and a walnut desk and a painting of a mother and child. A dish of newly-watered ivy. I sipped and waited for the warmth to remove the chill.

"Mothers," I muttered.

"Oh," said Miss Rodriguiz, smiling that all-knowing smile. "You've found the villains, have you?"

"Don't tell me that your sociology excuses mothers who scar their children. Don't tell me that Gail's mother isn't destroying a brilliant mind. You can't dispute that."

"Okay. Gail's mother was deserted by her husband before Gail was born. She tried to abort and failed. She's suffering pangs of guilt. She's not so bright and she sees Gail's brain as a threat. She needs Gail. Do you want to blame her? Blame the runaway husband who probably had an overprotective mother and never learned to take his responsibilities."

She was so glib. And so irritating.

"Then tell me," I said, "that Baby's mother is a saint for preventing that innocent from having an abortion. The child was probably raped. She doesn't even know the facts of life. She can't even go out with boys for another year."

"Who told you she was raped?"

"It's obvious."

"Little girls love to play house. She played in the wrong house. And she didn't get aborted because Mother wants that baby. Mother may let her have the dog but she wants a new love object in return. Especially with the divorce still hurting her ego."

"You can't mean it."

"Maybe I don't mean it. Why don't you listen to me? There are no pat answers, except in your textbooks. And the only conclusions come in novels which some teachers teach as gospel."

"Then prove to me that something didn't drive Sara away. A prize scholar and a model student doesn't run off with a wayward bus driver for no reason. There has to be cause and effect. Just show me the logic."

"You're aggravating," she said. "You want life so neat, and it just doesn't work out that way. Forget about Sara. You've lost your objectivity. I'll give you a case history. Here is a Jewish girl. We get relatively few Jewish girls. Her father's entire family is wiped out by the Germans. He was pulled almost dead from a covered trench. A very religious man. He came to this country and married a wife who died in childbirth and left him a daughter. He called her Shana, Shana the *beautiful*. He lavished every attention on the child. She was educated and became a teacher. And after a vacation she came to her fond papa pregnant by a German ski-bum. Did she keep the secret? Did she go off to a holiday in Switzerland to get herself a silent abortion? No. She told her father everything. Almost destroyed him. And now that the baby is delivered she's giving it up for adoption. Now tell me, is she a thankless child? I met the father myself. He's a decent sort. There's your cause and effect. You're an English teacher. Write me a conclusion." She took a sip of her cold coffee and turned her attention to her clipboard notes.

"What makes you so sure you're right?" I asked her. "What makes you so sure that your opinion is any more valid than mine? What happened to Baby is only your conjecture. You weren't there, were you? My conclusion could be just as right as yours."

She looked up from her papers. "When you know what it is that *you* want from Huntington House, you won't need to ask questions. Until then you'll have to be satisfied with somebody else's answers."

.

When the girls filed in for second period I was deep in thought. In a fantasy. I was pregnant. Why wouldn't I keep my secret from my loving father? I was Sara. Would anything as simple as a boring routine life send me flying to the arms of a vagrant? I was Baby. Would I have the nerve to let a boy get near me?

Sara didn't take her window seat. She moved to a table, slowly, because of her great discomfort. Heather was growing, a big fat healthy baby curled so tight and secure inside her mother that for an instant it made me feel good to sense her there.

"You should have seen them," said Baby, huffing with her great weight into the room. "Mrs. Miller's guppies had babies. You never saw such tiny fish."

"We have an aquarium at home," said Sara matter-of-factly. "Very important fish. My father feeds them every morning.

Each one is allotted a certain number of grains of food. I think
he taught the fish to count." Her eyes drifted. "Did you ever see
a fish in a mountain pool jump out of the water to grab a bug?"
She stopped.

I was glad she had. Because whether or not anybody's problem had a resolution, we had been overtaken by time. Graduation was at hand. Their secondary educations had to be cere-
moniously concluded.

"If you'll hand in your papers," I told them, almost regretfully
I admit, "we'll have to start planning the graduation." Regretfully because I needed more time.

Slowly the papers came in my direction. Sara handed hers
briskly forward. I took it with ambiguous feelings. Finally a
completed paper from Sara. But the doves on her balcony cooed
untended.

"It's a good paper," Sara said as I looked at it. "Very logical
and very well organized. But I have no intention of joining your
ceremony. So just count me out."

Such a flat statement. Her expression was flat, no buoyancy,
trapped by the magnet of the earth which pulled her down to it.
Such a pity.

"I thought you might borrow a guitar and play some music for
us, at least."

"If you can find a guitar I'll play something," she said, looking
directly at me, "but I'm not graduating. They can drag me home
if they want to, but they won't have the satisfaction of seeing me
graduate."

Gail rose from her chair, astonished and distressed. "Are you
going home? Aren't you going back to the mountains?"

"Aren't you going to nurse by the river?" whimpered Baby.
"Aren't you going to have a cradle of rushes?"

"Won't she play with the yearlings?" begged Marlene.

"How can I go to the mountains?" asked Sara, looking angrily at me. "I have to be practical. I have to think about ophthalmologists. I have to think about stomach disorders and mattresses with four hundred coils."

No! I wouldn't let her do that to me! I would not be responsible for her life! Exactly what I wanted to avoid! Her eyes pressed me with their accusations.

"Sara," I said in front of the class, unable to help myself, "I didn't mean . . ."

But her look had softened. "Don't worry. Don't think it's you. It's just logic. That's what education teaches you, isn't it? That's why you come to class and read the words on the page and write the papers and add the numbers. To be civilized and logical. We're not animals after all. We're social beings. And we have to follow rules."

Were those my words or theirs?

"We have to be responsible with the lives of others," she went on painfully. "We can be free with our own but when we have the lives of others we have to show concern. If we love her."

Baby was almost in tears. "You aren't going to have your back sling and take her hiking in Bryce Canyon at just evening when the shadows are coming?"

"There isn't any diaper service in Bryce Canyon. And the deep woods are too far from a telephone."

Gail covered her ears with her hands. "There are all sorts of rocks, all sorts of sirens' songs. Stop your ears! Please!"

"That's the right thing to do," said Mary Lou. "God knows what's good for us. God doesn't want us to be wild and sinful."

"You and your damn Jesus!" exploded Sara. "You can just take him and do you know what! So pinned to the cross and suffering! That's all your generation knows! Your generation doesn't even know that God is in the forest playing his pipes for us to dance!"

"That's the devil!" protested Mary Lou, moving away from Sara. "She's been tempted and she cursed God. I'm not standing next to her when something happens. She's going to get it."

"Please, everybody, try to cool down. It's hot and you're all getting close and you're nervous. I know how you feel. But we have to find a graduation theme. There's no avoiding it. It's time."

"We have a theme," said a pallid Gail. "Janus. The two-headed god of yesterday and tomorrow. He looks back in horror on yesterday and with astonishment at tomorrow."

"Then let it be Janus," I said. As good as any. "But let's delete horror and astonishment. Can you find anything less editorial?"

Golda opened our door, waved at Cookie. "Shana came back! She stole her own baby from the hospital and she's keeping it, and her father's here. Boy, is there going to be something!"

She headed toward the stairs and the class rose to follow.

"The graduation!" I called. Not very loudly. I wanted also to see this beautiful Shana. I wanted to see one climax, one conclusion. Sara walked beside me and I had to slow my steps for her.

"You said you knew how we felt," she said as we descended. "Tell me, what do you know?"

"I know how you feel about Heather."

"Who's Heather?" she asked emptily.

"What do you *mean* who's Heather!"

"I can't logically predict the sex of an unborn child, can I?"

I caught her by the arm. "Sara, that's so cruel . . ."

She pulled away. "You want logic, don't you? I once won a prize for making a machine that could detect radiation. Maybe when I get back to Omaha I can make a new machine that will empty all the stupid dreams out of my heart."

Beware the Enemy

THE GIRLS were already clustered around the mother and child when Sara and I reached the visitors' room. Sara went directly to the baby, lifted it from its mother's arms and pressed it to her own shoulder. As naturally as if she had done it a thousand times. And Heather was as real as the baby she held. I had pictured Heather myself, paddling in mountain streams, cooing in a bower of rushes. And what jolted me was that the materialization of Heather had happened quite without my realizing it. To dematerialize the Heather of the forests was unthinkable.

I also realized that this was the first baby I had seen at Huntington House, the first baby that belonged to the moans and groans and complaints. An actual exquisite baby. A tiny blond thing with tiny fists and a sleeping face furrowed in some primitive dream, a tiny mouth making little animal sucking motions.

"This is a teacher too," said Baby, pulling me over to Shana. And she returned to gaze at the infant in Sara's arms.

Shana made her explanation to me as the girls ogled the sleeping infant. "Just couldn't do it. I never should have looked at him. He grabbed me, that's all. If I can find a place to stay for a while until I'm stronger, I'll figure out how to handle it." She looked gray and desperate. "The best-laid plans," she said.

"Smell this baby!" called Sara from the center of the group. "He smells like mushrooms in the damp earth."

"He needs a dinner and a bath," said Shana, looking anxiously toward Miss Rodriguiz' office. "Why don't they come out of there."

"I hope you're nursing!" called Sara.

"I'm trying but he bites," laughed Shana. Her laughter disappeared with Miss Rodriguiz' voice.

"Come into the office for a minute, Shana. I think we've got you some temporary housing."

"I don't want to come in for a minute. Just ask him to leave a little money so that I can survive. I don't want to offend his eyes. And I don't want my little bastard to offend his name and his God."

Behind Miss Rodriguiz appeared a man, tall, gaunt, dark like his daughter, anger set in the lines of his face.

"I won't let her starve. I won't throw her in some ditch to die. I left her the money."

He strode toward the door. "Let me pass," he said gruffly as he moved through the cluster of girls. Sara rose from her chair, lifted the baby toward Shana, let the blanket fall from the baby's face.

"Here's your son, Shana."

The grandfather tried to avert his eyes, but they saw the baby. And once they had seen it they were trapped. He stopped, stared at the tiny sleeping figure.

"It's a baby," said Shana, "what fallen women have."

His eyes fastened on the child, attracted beyond his ability to turn away, mesmerized, frozen.

"It's a little German," said Shana. "He's unclean. You don't want him."

The man pulled the child roughly from Sara's arms, forced her to relinquish it, fell into a chair staring at the baby. The infant awakened, began to cry, a thin cry like an animal's.

"He doesn't want you," said Sara. "He's not loved by you and he doesn't need you. Give Shana her son."

He clutched the baby as it wailed, looking at his daughter's tired face, trying to remember something, holding tight to the screaming baby, forming the words soundlessly before he spoke.

"I thought God had deserted me. I thought this was the last plague. Praise God in His infinite wisdom, Shana, it was a gift." He began to weep onto the weeping baby.

Shana passed a hand over her face, no more strength left in her. "He's not a gift, Poppa. He's not your salvation. And I'm not your salvation. When are you going to realize that? When are you going to stop leeching on my life? When are you going to let me go?"

Miss Rodriguiz was making notes on her clipboard.

"He's German, Poppa. He's the enemy."

"God in His infinite mercy," he wept, "took away my family and used the seed of the enemy to replant my fields. Shana, my beautiful, come home."

He lifted the baby and started for the door. The crying of the child floated after him.

Shana dragged herself out of the chair.

"Is this the way you want it?" asked Miss Rodriguiz. "It's your choice."

"He's not going to build his life on my son the way he built it on mine," she said bitterly. "It's too heavy." She followed her father and her son. "I'll just stay a little while until I rest up," she said. She turned to me. "It's expedient," she explained, almost apologetically. The door closed behind her.

Most of the girls drifted away.

"Neat?" asked Miss Rodriguiz. She returned to her office. And only Sara and Gail and I remained. Sara sat shivering on the sofa.

"That's what they'll do to me," she said, horrified. "They'll take all the air away from her. They'll leech on her and squeeze her into their shape. She won't be free at all! They won't harbor her the way they say! They'll smother her!"

Gail put her hands up to her ears. "Don't say it," she pleaded.

"Gail is right. You can't compare Shana's situation to yours. It's not the same thing."

"And if I take her away there aren't any pediatricians in the woods. Oh God, I can't keep her!" The thought of it cut through her and she winced with a pain as sharp as labor. "I'll have to give her away to make her free!"

A cry came from Gail such as I'd never heard from her. "No!" she wailed. "Someone has to conquer the maze! Someone has to get out!" She walked unsteadily from the room, her words still audible down the hall. "Somebody has to win!"

Exactly what I had feared. I never should have spoken my mind to her. "You don't mean you'd give up your baby! When I suggested it I didn't know how you felt about Heather. You just can't do it!"

"But it's the only thing *to* do! It's like writing a topic sentence. All the other sentences are linked together. They're all one piece. What you said was right. Don't be upset." She stroked my arm to comfort me. "You told me what was true and it was true."

"True for me but not for you! I only told you what *I* would do. You aren't *me!*"

"Who says I'm not," she answered simply.

·

I called J. at least four times that evening. He wasn't home. Odd that he wasn't home on a week night. Not that it made any difference. I just wondered where he was on a week night. So late.

Practice Makes Perfect

THIS BETTER BE RIGHT," said Helen, handing us the master stencil of the typed graduation program. "It took me a whole morning and I want my credit."

"It's a beautiful program," said Doris, reading the copy carefully. "You're to be congratulated for such a conscientious job. I see that you have Sara participating but not graduating and Mary Lou graduating but not participating."

"Amazing," said the old secretary, "that Sara decided to relinquish. That's one I never expected. But of course she's made the right decision."

"And the subject Janus," said Doris. "There won't be anything offensive to those who are religious? To have a pagan deity as a subject for a graduation address?"

"There is nothing to offend the ears of the most devout. Gail wrote a fine speech in spite of the fact that she hasn't been feeling well. Did the gowns arrive?"

"I picked them up from the Salvation Army this morning. Most gracious and generous to lend them to us. I left them in the living room."

"And you've arranged for that retired teacher to speak and bring along some of her poetry."

"The poor thing died," said the old secretary. 'I was ever so sorry to hear it."

"So we were *fortunate*," emphasized Doris, "to get a last-minute speaker from Downtown."

"*Downtown!* I won't have it! I'm not going to have my graduation spoiled by a professional coffee-break educator!"

Doris rose tall, crossed her arms in serene control. "This is not *your* graduation. This is *their* graduation. And our speaker is very sought after, and we are *honored* that he thinks enough of our educational program to address us."

"I'm not going to retype the program!" yelled Helen.

"And it's possible that Mary Lou will be able to participate. Nurse Caulfield says that she's feeling quite well. So perhaps you can just retype that small portion."

"I won't do it," complained Helen.

"Just once more," I pleaded with her. "I'll give you double credit."

"It better be the last," she muttered, "or else."

"And don't be so nervous," Doris advised me.

"I'm not nervous, Doris. I just want this graduation to go smoothly. The girls have been upset all week. Gail and Sara are very close and all the girls were counting on Sara's baby. They all seem so let down."

"These are the problems of teaching in a maternity home. You might consider them before you decide whether to return in the fall."

Decide?

Annabelle came stamping into the office. "My homemaking class absolutely refuses to make the graduation refreshments. They claim that the refreshments are part of their grade and they found out that the report cards are already marked so they won't make the finger sandwiches for no credit."

"But we've been planning on the refreshments! They've worked so hard on this graduation in spite of the fact that they feel rotten. And I want it to be nice for them."

"Mrs. Vanderveld had a lovely graduation last year," said Doris. "She always handled these things beautifully and graciously."

"I'm meeting the girls in the living room for the rehearsal. And it will be beautiful because they are beautiful. I just hope your speaker from Downtown knows what he's doing."

"We *are* nervous aren't we," she said as she turned to leave.

.

Annabelle followed me to the living room. "Actually," she said, "Mrs. Vanderveld had diabetes and she fainted during the ceremony. And don't worry" — she squeezed my arm in her massive grasp — "my girls will come through. Even if I have to make two hundred finger sandwiches myself. Doris is just jealous."

"Jealous! Of what?"

"The girls like you. You're edging in on her territory. It took her two years to get used to Clara Vanderveld."

.

The seniors were already in the living room when I arrived, shuffling through the pile of blue and white robes on the living room table.

"Look at these dirty dickies," wailed Cookie. "I'm not going to graduate in a dirty dickey! I didn't study hard for three whole years just to graduate in a dirty dickey!"

"When was all this?" asked Gail. Her face had broken out in some sort of raw, splotchy rash. "When did you do all this studying?"

"You shouldn't make fun of me," said Cookie. "I have credits on my records for three years. You haven't got any more credits than I have."

"It's true," said Gail, pulling at her lip. "Janus has two heads. Both of them are laughing at me." She turned her eyes to Sara who sat silently strumming her guitar in the corner of the room.

"This robe is a mile too long." Baby giggled as she stepped on the blue material. "Can somebody make it shorter?"

"And me!" laughed Marlene.

Cookie turned this way and that in her gown. "I look like a tub in a sheet."

She did. "Arch forward," I advised her. "Let the folds fall from the bust. It will sort of drape over your stomach."

"Lean to your left," said Gail. "Your left bust is larger."

"Why don't you *stop* it," said Cookie. "You're getting so mean!"

Gail recoiled, looked for comfort at Sara whose graduation song floated, thin and mournful, though the complaints.

> *I look at life from both sides now,*
> *It's life's illusions I recall*
> *I really don't know life . . . at all . . .*

"Can't you make Sara graduate with us?" begged Baby. "I want Heather to graduate with me. I miss Heather."

Sara must have been listening. She threw her hair back away from her face, shot Baby a scalding glance. Baby protested to me with her eyes.

"It's tomorrow. And I want this one rehearsal without music. Tomorrow morning there will be a professional pianist but today I'll just bang out the music on the piano and let's try marching into the sun room the way we plotted it out."

I turned once more to Sara who sat strumming and humming, her head bent so low over her guitar that her face was once more obscured. Yet I knew that she was listening. The girls were beginning to line up in order, Baby leading the uncertain procession.

"Come on, Sara," I asked her. "Won't you change your mind?

We've been together all semester. Come on and join us now for the final ceremony."

"Why?" she answered through her hair. "What's the use."

"All right then. Chests high. Just think of it this way. Left together right, left together right." I thumped my tum-tum-di-tum-tum on the piano. "And try not to be so mechanical. Just pause slightly and touch a toe and advance."

Sara laughed from her corner, shaking her wild hair. "You look like a bunch of rhinos on the way to the water hole."

"I wish you would come," Gail pleaded. "I need you." She looked wretched. But Sara just returned to her strumming.

"Baby is starting on the wrong foot," complained Helen. "She always messes up the line." Baby whimpered.

"And don't sway when you pause," I advised Cookie.

"I don't sway. It sways. And I'm going to wash this dirty dickey."

"Indeed you won't," Doris corrected her from the doorway. She stood with a frightened girl, almost as tall as Doris, huge bulging eyes, faintly pregnant, clutching bony fingers in nervous anguish. "The Salvation Army has graciously consented to lend us these robes and we are particularly requested not to wash them. No water is to touch the dickies. You may press them but you may not wash them. And this is Zelda, who wants to graduate with us. I'm sure you can find her a small part in the graduation."

"I'm not going to retype the program!" exploded Helen. "I won't touch it again!"

Zelda shrank back as Doris left her, fearful to enter the strange group.

"Come on in, Zelda. We'll find a part for you. And if you all want to wash the dickies, wash them. There's no word in the Bible against putting water on dickies. So wash them. I give you permission."

"Finally," said Sara from her corner, "your generation has taken a stand." Her words were mocking but her voice was without recrimination. "You're the dickey-washer of your generation. I'm proud of you."

"I'm back," came a voice from the doorway. "I'm graduating. I'm married." Mary Lou stood holding a pillow, her hair immaculately and intricately piled, her stomach almost flat.

"What happened?" screamed the girls, surrounding her. Sara dropped her guitar and came to hear the news.

"My son is baptized Catholic. I don't care what his mother wants. It's done."

"How did you get him to marry you?" asked Cookie. "Did you make him?"

"God did it. I have to sit on a pillow because of my stitches. I have fourteen stitches. It's part of my penance."

Sara stood beside her, searching her face. "Are you happy?" she asked desperately. "Do you love him?"

"He's sent off to fight the enemy," said Mary Lou.

"What enemy?" asked Gail.

"He's working in the store. The fighting men need their provisions when they go out to fight godless Communism. It's God's will."

"I don't care if the program isn't right," said Helen. "You can use it the way it is. It keeps changing every minute."

"Make Sara graduate," whimpered Baby. "If Heather doesn't graduate then I don't want to."

"Me neither," said Marlene. "Heather wants to. I know it."

"For God's sake," pleaded Sara, "there isn't any Heather. This is a strange baby I don't even know! She's somebody else's. I'm going to have her blindfolded so I don't ever have to see her. And don't talk about her anymore, please!"

"Not *her*," said Gail pointedly. "*It*. If you don't believe in Heather then say *it*."

"Shit *it!*" said Sara running from the room, almost colliding with a terribly old lady in a thin paisley dress. Her white hair in a faint net. Her long skeletal fingers trembling in my direction to catch my attention.

"Please," she asked, "would you prefer 'A Pretty Girl Is Like a Melody' or 'Pomp and Circumstance' at a faster tempo?"

"I beg pardon?"

"I'm your pianist. Would you like 'A Pretty Girl Is Like a Melody' or 'Pomp and Circumstance' for your exit?"

"Try the 'Battle Hymn of the Republic,'" said Gail, dropping her gown and heading out to Sara.

"I'd better get my credit," said Helen, "or there's going to be trouble around here."

·

J. not at home. Not at two in the morning. Not at three. It is too cruel. Drowning. Help.

Parturition Day

BABY stumbled down the stairs in her heels, or rather in Cookie's heels, her painted face like a little girl playing grownup on Halloween.

"Did my mother come yet?" she asked anxiously.

"I don't know, Baby. I'm just going into the sun room to see who's there. Tell the others to gather in the living room as soon as they're ready."

"You look so pretty," she said to me. It was greatly appreciated. *Greatly* appreciated. "Call me if my mother comes," she begged.

The office was splendid with flowers and the sun room, with its rows of wooden chairs neatly arranged, was marred only by the lack of sun, which could not quite get through the dusty windows. The room was beginning to fill with guests. Two nuns in dark habits sat in the rear, chatting and laughing together. Three tall, athletic boys were crowded at the side of the room, leaning toward each other as they talked, laughing and smacking each other energetically, overflowing the chairs that didn't quite hold them. Across the laps of two was a huge package ornately done in purple and silver paper and fastened with an enormous purple flower.

Doris in her navy suit, relieved only by her already wilted

corsage, waved a stack of diplomas at me. "Be sure to tell your girls that their diplomas will be mailed to them from their home schools."

"What do you mean *mailed?* What's that you're holding?"

"Diploma *covers.* Don't worry. It's always done this way."

"Do you *mean* that they go through the entire ceremony and you hand them nothing but an empty cover?"

"They may keep the tassels on their hats. I assure you that the girls would be more disappointed not to be able to keep their tassels than to have to wait for their diplomas."

I tried to sort out the logic.

"And I hope that when you thank the speaker you take into consideration how much it means to us to have a man from Downtown here at Huntington House. It is a real feather in our cap."

Ada walked in, scanned the room to see if any enemy was present, took a corner seat, her face as angry as when I last saw her. But in her hand was a small wrapped package.

A pale, slender woman in a knit suit came in carrying a box with a puppy in it. A Dalmatian puppy. The puppy was sleeping. The nuns came forward to pet it.

Sara's father and mother entered, holding hands and smiling. I had to tell them. "Sara won't take part in the graduation. She's going to sing, but she will not march."

"Don't worry," her father said confidently, "she'll be all right."

A woman with long red hair, cut and styled too young for her face, headed toward me.

"Gail still gonna make the speech?"

"Yes, she is," I assured her. "She's our major speaker."

She frowned in disapproval. "She's due. You shouldn't make her work so close to her date. They don't know what's good for them. I hope I can get her nose out of a book long enough to have the baby."

Our librarian entered with a stack of gifts in his hands. Books, from the shape of them. He blew me a kiss.

The other girls began to fill the room, dressed in their best, scrubbed and polished, wearing clean smocks. Miss Rodriguiz took her seat. Annabelle and Nurse Caulfield and the old secretary and Lucy from the kitchen. Dr. Lewin without his white coat. Other people I didn't know looking self-consciously about them.

The room was becoming hot and sticky. Someone flicked on the air conditioner. The blower started with a roar, mixed with the hubbub in the room. My seniors in the living room would be hot and uncomfortable under the gowns. I went to join them.

Helen was peering through a crack in the sun room door, looking for a face.

"Your mother is here," I told her.

"I *know* that," she said impatiently, bitter disappointment that it was only Ada.

Sara stepped into the room in an old T-shirt pulled over openbuttoned jeans. "All right!" she shouted. "All right! I'll graduate! That's what you wanted, isn't it!"

"She will," screamed Baby, clapping her hands.

Gail came up and embraced her.

"There's a gown in my closet upstairs," I told her. I had washed the dickey myself.

"I *know* it's there!" she said angrily.

"We're almost ready to start. Will you have time?"

"That's all your generation thinks of," she said. "Time. What the hell good is time!" Gail trailed after her through the door.

Baby turned around for me to see her. "I'm hemmed," she said. "Did my mother come?"

"She's here," I answered.

She clasped her fat hands together, almost in a prayer. "Did she say anything about my dog?"

"She brought it with her. In a box."

Such joy radiated from her face, such a smile from one fat cheek to the other. "Is it a Dalmatian?" she whispered prayerfully.

"With spots," I answered.

Marlene hugged her. The others crowded in, wiping the tears that cut roads under Cookie's heavy powder.

Baby hugged her stomach. "My baby will play with him. My baby will have a friend."

"I think my gown is too short," whispered Zelda apologetically. It came to her ankles. "And my hair won't curl."

"Don't worry," said Cookie. "After the graduation I'll teach you to fix yourself up. How come your eyes are so funny?"

"I have a thyroid problem," said Zelda.

"I'll show you how to paint on a beauty mark so people won't look so much at your bulgy eyes."

Sara stalked into the room, her dickey hastily tied and sticking out. She had not changed her pants. The cuffs were evident under the gown. But her hair was brushed. She was beautiful. Gail, smiling beside her, was beautiful. So were they all, all beautiful.

"Let's go already," moaned Cookie. "I'm melting."

I peered through the crack. All the seats in my range of vision were filled. I looked toward the piano. The old pianist and her old page-turner were poised and waiting. She in velvet. He in a baggy dinner jacket. In all that heat.

"This is it. Line up."

They rose from chairs and sofas, visibly nervous, straightened their mortarboards, arranged their gowns. Beautiful all. I would probably cry.

The old pianist lifted her bony fingers over the keys, an elegant droop to the wrists. The turner, leaning on a cane, reached trembling fingers toward the page. I opened the doors to the sun room. Doris ran in, slammed them.

"What are you doing!"

"We're graduating."

"The speaker from Downtown isn't here yet!"

"Then I'm sorry for the speaker. We have a good program without him. I don't want my seniors fainting under these hot gowns. So get ready," I called to them. "This is it!"

Doris threw her bony frame against the door, barred it like a colossus. "You will not start until the speaker comes!"

"Seniors," I said, as resolutely as she, "get ready!"

"Get her!" called Helen gleefully.

A beefy face poked into the living room, glossy hair parted in the center, a practiced smile, a black bow tie. It could be no other. "Sorry to be late, ladies. You can start."

I opened the door. I waved to the pianist. Doris floated out after the speaker from Downtown. The frail fingers of the pianist descended in a crescendo. The girls raised their bosoms.

It had begun. Like a pregnancy. What had been conceived on the day I entered Huntington House had come to its inevitable conclusion. I checked them. They were grand. Poised. In control. They smiled at me. All but Sara. But what she told me with her unsmiling eyes was a novel, full of metaphors.

The starting note. I handed Baby forward, down the aisle. I stood beside them, let each girl step out as the next stepped forward, perfect cadence. Step, together, step. They arrived at the front of the sun room, turned neatly, stood each before a wooden armchair. With a hand I stopped the music. With a hand I lowered the girls. There was silence, and the whirr of the air conditioner. With a finger I raised Baby. She walked to the microphone, carefully looked at the little card she held in her hand. Studied it to make certain the words were right.

"Will the audience please rise and salute the flag," she intoned.

Respectfully the audience rose. Behind me a soft voice asked, "Is there a seat for me or can I just stand here and watch?"

A boy. No, a man. Gentle tired eyes, watery blue, sun-reddened from the road. A dirty pullover shirt and jeans. Softly he asked again, "Is it okay if I sit down or shall I just stand back here?"

The audience was pledging. I pointed him a seat behind the three great fellows. Sara couldn't possibly see him. But I had. From the look of him he was not in a position to pay a pediatrician. But neither was he the wild boy I imagined. And I knew that Heather would have blue eyes.

I had taken my attention from the performance. When I returned, a frantic Baby was waiting for a cue. I raised a finger toward her grateful face. She consulted her card once more. With a smile of satisfaction at a job well done, she intoned, "Will the audience please be seated."

As Unaccustomed as I Am

WHEN I SEE these girls here today," intoned the speaker, his thumbs casually hooked in his vest pocket, "I know how lucky they are that their mothers and fathers and all you good people here in this audience stood by them through their misfortune. But these girls are fortunate, *fortunate*, that the education was available to them in their hour of need. And they should be proud of themselves that they had the stick-to-itiveness to finish their school work, in spite of trials and tribulations, and proud of the folks who stuck by them."

Applause. Somebody actually *applauded*.

"And I know that every one of these girls sitting up here today is filled with a sense of gratitude and a sense of obligation."

Nurse Caulfield touched my shoulder. "Where did they find this creep? Why is he trying to make them feel guilty?"

"*Downtown*," I said. Doris leaned over and poked me, hard.

The girls didn't hear him. They were self-absorbed, interior, crossing and recrossing their ankles, trying to find a comfortable place for their hands.

"I remember during the war," he reminisced, "the last war, the *good* war, we had some Mexican fellows working on the base. They couldn't speak English. Well, we officers felt a sense of obligation to educate these fellows and teach them English. So we set up schools on the base. And believe me, these Mexicans were grateful for what we did. We have letters" — he tapped his jacket pocket — "telling us how grateful they were. And that's the way these girls feel today. They have put their shoulders to the wheel and persevered and today they find themselves at their graduation, one of the greatest moments of their lives."

I had heard enough. I tuned him out and turned my attention to the boy from the VW bus. A thin pale boy, in no way able to fight the father from Omaha. In no way able to tame the raging current that was about to engulf him. He sat staring, not at the speaker but at Sara.

I was jolted by applause. Without waiting for my cue Sara had pushed her chair up to the microphone. Her thin clear voice subdued the audience. The strings of her guitar plucked poignant chords, as moving in their simplicity and clarity as the words she sang.

> *I look at life from both sides now*
> *From win and lose*
> *But still somehow*
> *It's life's illusions I recall*
> *I really don't know life, at all.*

I watched the boy as she sang. He hunched forward, thin shouldered, looking at her between the bodies of the big boys in front of him. He was weeping silently.

Gail waited for my cue because she was nervous. She wiped her face on the arm of her robe. Sara touched her gently on the shoulder to reassure her before pulling her own chair back to the graduates' row. Gail turned to Sara for strength. And then stood alone, her eyes not on her audience but on me, asking me also for strength. I smiled at her.

"Janus," she began in a faltering voice, "is a two-headed god. We've all seen pictures of his faces. He looks forward to tomorrow at the same time he looks backward to yesterday. In the same way we here today look to both at once. To the yesterday that brought us here, the yesterday that saw the beginnings of our educations, and to the tomorrow that holds for us what we hope will be hope."

It crossed her face just then, like the snake of a tremor. She was in labor. I looked to Nurse Caulfield who looked at me. "I'll bet it is," she said. "But don't worry. She has hours to go."

Gail began to perspire, pulling at her lip, looking toward the place where her mother was seated.

"Janus," she stumbled on, rambling, ". . . time and place are in confusion . . . we are in a vague place where life is being created . . . we are the instrument and we are acted upon . . . we are a duality . . ."

The audience sat polite, shook their heads, yes.

"We are a conundrum," she said, completely out of touch with her speech, ". . . yesterday and tomorrow are one . . . we are at one with our babies . . . we are the bearer and we are the borne . . ."

The audience shuffled uncomfortably, left behind by her disoriented rhetoric. "We are the Father and the Son and the Holy Ghost, we are the Trinity, it is joined here together." She pressed her stomach. "We are holy and yet the Philistines press in on us and make us profane. What's most sublime becomes a nightmare and what's most holy becomes an act of shame. We are enmeshed. Trapped in time and space."

The audience fidgeted and coughed. Sara leaned forward, tugged at her gown. Gail shuddered, and then awoke, and then picked up the thread of her speech.

"Yesterday is past and tomorrow is yet to come. We have opportunities waiting for us tomorrow, opportunities in education and opportunities to make something useful of ourselves."

The audience relaxed, settled back to hear a proper graduation speech, folded hands, fanned themselves with programs.

When the girls rose to receive their diploma cases, the audience sighed. When the tassels were moved, they wept, some audibly. And then "A Pretty Girl Is Like a Melody." The graduates marched out amid congratulations and relieved laughter. And the whole crowd filled the living room, hugging and talking, milling and greeting.

I could see a frantic Gail being maneuvered by her mother to the door. She pulled toward me, her mother dragging behind her.

"Will you come!" her mother scolded. "Do I have to tell you again? Are you listening to me?"

"Don't let Sara go home," Gail begged me. "Don't let her give Heather away to them. Make her stronger than we are!"

Sara had made her way through the press, pushed the mother aside to embrace Gail. But the embrace was a recognition of finality. Gail took Sara's arms solemnly. "Hail and farewell," she said. "If we do not meet again, this was a parting well made."

"Will you *come!*" ordered her mother. Gail was hauled off, through the crowd.

"Please!" Gail shouted back to us. "Somebody has to get away!" A few heads turned in her direction. "Some of us have to get out before they lock the doors!" And she was lost from view. The partying continued and the ripples of voices filled the place where the plea had echoed.

I turned back to Sara but she was gone. I looked for the boy. Sara stood with her parents and the two nuns. No one else.

Baby interrupted my search with a puppy, curled in her arms, nesting in the blue warmth of her robe. She raised it to let me touch the furry ears with a finger. "I'll love it forever," she said reverently. "I'm only sad Heather couldn't see it."

They pressed around me. From the sun room I saw the boy enter. He must have been still in his seat, waiting, or thinking. Or just frightened. Or reluctant. I saw him work his way through the crowd toward Sara and her parents.

Doris pushed beside me, the speaker from Downtown on her arm. "And this is our new English teacher. It was she who prepared the lovely graduation."

"It was swell," he boomed. "Really swell. You're doing a swell job."

I turned my eyes from him to Sara who saw the boy. Her face opened like a flower, took him in all at once, and then fell in agony.

"I only hope my poor little speech didn't take the edge off the speeches of those wonderful brave girls," smiled the speaker.

"Don't worry," I said. "It didn't. Your speech stank."

A Functional Change

THE BOY slumped wearily in a chair, just watching Sara with those pale eyes.

"I don't see why *she* needs to be here," said Sara's father, motioning his head in my direction.

"Because I want her here," said Sara, holding on to my arm. Her eyes darted from her parents to the boy who, as far as I had noted, hadn't said a single word to her.

"She's my friend. I can have at least one friend to defend me, can't I?"

"This isn't a trial," said Miss Rodriguiz. "And this is your English teacher, not a witness." She tapped her clipboard with her pencil, warned me with her eyes not to be unprofessional. "What's your position here?" she asked me. "A teacher or a friend?"

Sara held me tight, made her urgent request with her fingers. And I held her hand in return. Something I think I had never done before.

"I think I'm here as a friend," I said.

Sara's tense hand relaxed and she turned her full attention to the boy who sat silent and uncomfortable. She was trying to find something in his face.

"Hi," she said finally.

"Hi," he answered, letting his eyes search her face also, and then dropping his eyes to her full ripe stomach. She opened her gown, exposing the bulging T-shirt for him to see.

"Sara Jean," warned her mother. "Stop it."

The boy leaned forward in his chair, reached tentative fingers toward her, toward the tight pouch where his baby curled, ran his fingers lovingly over the shape of it.

"Do you see what he's doing?" cried Sara's mother. "We've talked all this over. Now he's luring her back. Wake up, Sara Jean!" Her voice was more a command than a plea. "In half an hour you would have been gone. It's just luck that he turned up when he did. Is that what you want for your baby? Luck? Chance?"

Sara turned to her mother. Searched that face also.

"You're out of your mind," said her father. "Sara, if you had no baby I'd understand. But not with a child to consider. Are you going to deliver this baby at the side of a road somewhere? Are you going to let strangers cut the cord for you?"

"Sara," pleaded her mother. "Consider what you're doing. You have a responsibility to this child. When you bear a child life changes. You just can't run off to the woods. When you have a child you pledge to give up a part of your freedom. That's the price. And is this the man who is going to protect you and your child? Will he give up a part of *his* freedom for you?"

Something in her mother's words nagged at her, tore at her.

"Don't badger her if she wants to be a fool," said her father. He turned to the boy. "Just tell her. Are you willing right now to go out and get a job in a store? In a bank? Sweeping oil in a gas station to pay for that baby? Are you ready to give up this wild life you call freedom? Just tell Sara Jean. Are you ready to give it up?"

The boy had an exceedingly gentle voice. "I'm not ready. I

have things to do. And I have things to see. But I want Sara to see them with me. I came back for her."

"You can't be such a fool," said the father to his daughter. "If you do you'll have a bitter lesson to learn from your own experience."

"I won't let her ruin herself!" said Sara's mother. "I've put too many years of my own life into that girl to let her be blown away! Like chaff! Think," she pleaded with Sara, "think of the dear baby. Think of when you were little. Your asthma. Do you remember how we suffered with you? Lord knows we took our responsibility! And now it's time for you to take yours. When you couldn't breathe, remember Sara Jean? Who is going to run for the doctor in the middle of the night in the dark woods when your baby is choking!"

Sara choked at her mother's words, reaching to her own throat in agony, breathed heavily at the pull of the ancient asthma. Then she turned again to the boy, met his eyes full and open.

"All right!" said the mother bitterly. "Take him! Have him! But you can't have the baby too! Give it up as you've planned! Let someone who cares take care of it! You make the choice! You can't have him and the baby too! You *have* to make the choice!"

Sara looked at me and then back to the boy. "It isn't an *it*," she said. "It's a girl. And her name is Heather. And I love her. And I want her."

All he did was nod his head.

"Another half hour!" shrieked the mother, "and we would have been gone and he'd never see you again. Then it would be another Sara and another mountain and another woman's baby!"

Sara paused in purgatory, in limbo, swaying to the boy and then to the logic of the father, choking with a moment of remembrance, seeing the boy's soft face, hearing her mother. And then she turned to me.

"You tell me what you feel!" she said to me. "Tell me what you feel!"

She caught me in confusion. Not I. Not again. Not for the world. Not for anything would I tell her what to do. I choked with her old asthma.

"Watch yourself," warned Miss Rodriguiz.

"Sara," I said as she waited for my answer, "I can't make this decision for you."

"I didn't ask you to tell me what to *do!*" Her voice softened as she reached to me. "I just asked you to tell me what you *feel.*"

"Sara," I pleaded with her, "I can't answer for your life!"

"Yes, you can," she said. "You have to. If you can't, who can?"

"Sara, be sensible," said Miss Rodriguiz.

"Tell me what you feel," Sara persisted. "Sooner or later you have to join what's human, and what's human is all one. It's not in parts. And if I ask you to answer, that's how we join together. Don't just sit back and say to *whom* it may concern. It's to me, Sara. And it's to her, Heather. Tell me what you feel. Tell me now."

.

"So what did you tell her?" asked J. urgently. "What did you say?"

"Where were you?" I wept. "I tried to reach you for days!"

"I told you I was going out of town. You never listen to me. What did you tell her?"

"I blew it! It took me all semester to begin to understand what I was trying to do! Suddenly when I begin to see, when I finally begin to feel what sort of a thing is needed to be a teacher I blew it! It's more than a job! More than an art! And it's important to me. I want to stay there and I wrecked everything."

"What did you tell her?" begged J.

"They're threatening me with a lawsuit. And I'm probably fired for insulting that prick from Downtown. And it was so stupid! She was going with him anyway, no matter what I said."

"You told her to go!" He laughed.

"She would have gone anyway! And what if he deserts her? What if she has that baby in a ditch somewhere and she commits suicide? I'll feel guilty for the rest of my life! Maybe it wasn't enough that he loves her!"

"You told her to go!" cried J., with more joy than I had heard from him for a long time.

"Yes I told her to go! I told her to go with that foolish careless boy. Just tell me why I did it! Just explain to me how I could have done it!"

"I'll tell you why," said J., laughing like an idiot.

"I'll have the whole Board of Education on my neck. I'll lose my credential. It was a wild stupid thing to do."

"Yes," he laughed, "it was pretty wild and it was pretty stupid."

"Don't call me stupid," I said, "even if I am. Just tell me why, if you know so much."

"I do," said J. "I know so much. And I'm going to tell you how much I know. But honey, not on the phone. I'm coming over."

And so he did.